Echoes of
OPEN GLORY

Tales from Portrush and the
1951 Golf Championship

Maurice McAleese

ABOUT THE AUTHOR

Maurice McAleese is the author of *Back Through the Fields*, recalling old country characters and customs, published in 2005. His *Golden Strands* book (2009) tells the seaside story of Portrush where he was born and grew up. A third book, *Golden Days*, putting the same focus on Portstewart and its seaside history, appeared two years later.

An artist as well as a writer, his books are illustrated by many of his own sketches and paintings. He also writes short stories, some of which have been broadcast by the BBC, RTE and Downtown Radio. Others have been published in magazines and anthologies. A retired journalist, he and his wife, Thelma, live in Portstewart.

For the golfer within,
who always strikes the ball majestically
on the old imagined fairways.

Published 2014 by Colourpoint Books
an imprint of Colourpoint Creative Ltd
Colourpoint House, Jubilee Business Park
21 Jubilee Road, Newtownards, BT23 4YH
Tel: 028 9182 6339
Fax: 028 9182 1900
E-mail: info@colourpoint.co.uk
Web: www.colourpoint.co.uk

First Edition
First Impression

Designed by April Sky Design, Newtownards
Tel: 028 9182 7195
Web: www.aprilsky.co.uk

Printed by GPS Colour Graphics Ltd, Belfast

ISBN 978-1-78073-068-4

Front cover: Detail taken from the poster 'Golf in Northern
Ireland, The 8th Green at Portrush' painted by Norman
Wilkinson for the LMS Railway Company in 1924. The
location is in reality the famous 6th Green. (*National
Railway Museum/Science & Society Picture Library*)

Rear cover: Left – Golfers in front of the old Clubhouse at
Dunluce Avenue, which was in use until 1946.
Right – A busy summer scene at the Arcadia, Portrush.

CONTENTS

ACKNOWLEDGEMENTS

BETWEEN THE COVERS OF this book are echoes not only of The Open but also of many other old fairways and highways. Some are my own 'echoes of memory' and some are echoes of voices from past times that have inspired me on this particular journey.

Many of the words and thoughts, observations and quotations, have been culled from the archives of old newspapers, especially *The Northern Constitution* and *The Coleraine Chronicle*. Others have come from old holiday brochures and guide books.

A Portrush holiday guide book from the early 1950s and some other material relevant to the same era were made available to me by former work colleague, Stanley Bate, from his personal collection. Corrado Morelli allowed me to view an album of photographs from the 1995 British Seniors Open in Portrush at which Max Faulkner was present to see his son-in-law, Brian Barnes, lift the trophy. Some old golfing photographs were shown to me also by Charlie McConaghy.

Niall O'Boyle is now the custodian of the shoes worn by Max Faulkner when he won the 1951 Open, along with some other interesting memorabilia. He told me the story of how he came to have the famous shoes (he got Max Faulkner to autograph them when he was back in Portrush in 1995). Thanks to Niall I have been able to leave this very unusual 'footprint' in the book!

John McNally, a past Captain of Royal Portrush, and Rory Hamilton, a past President of the Rathmore Club gave me invaluable help.

Peter Alliss, who is very much regarded as the 'golden voice of golf', responded positively to my (perhaps cheeky!) request for some of his memories of the 1951 Open when, as a 21-year-old, he was just setting out on his distinguished career as a professional golfer.

Malcolm Johnston and his colleagues at Colourpoint Books, by their skill and professionalism, have done a superb job with the design and lay-out of the book, giving it a stunningly beautiful look and feel.

I very much like a quotation I came across recently which I think chimes nicely with its spirit and content. It's from the pen of the American author, Richelle E Goodrich:

> "Words never fade away but echo on for eternity. Let your echo ring sweet."

Whether or not you are a golfer, many 'echoes' from Portrush await you in these pages. I hope you will find all of them sweet!

FOLLOWING THROUGH:
ANOTHER MAJOR MILESTONE

Courtesy BBC NI

THE OLDEST AND MOST prestigious golf tournament in the world, The Open Championship, is returning to the Causeway Coast. This has been confirmed by the Championship's governing body, the R and A. It was last played over the famous Dunluce links at Royal Portrush in 1951 when the winner was the stylish and enigmatic Englishman, Max Faulkner. So when the first players step onto the first tee at Royal Portrush next time round (it could be in 2019) it will be a moment to savour, not only in the history of this old established Club, but also The Open itself.

The great Fred Daly, a famous son of Portrush, won the title in 1947 and Darren Clarke, who now lives in Portrush, brought the famed Claret Jug back to the town when he won the Championship in 2011.

With his stunning victory in the 2014 Open Championship at Hoylake, Holywood's Rory McIlroy must have felt the hand of history on his young shoulders. Rory also has strong links with Royal Portrush, where he holds the course record. He would have known that it was on this very course that Fred Daly had won this most coveted of golf trophies back in 1947, the first Ulsterman to do so.

In a holiday guide from the 1950s, Portrush is described as "a place where golfers foregather". That 'foregathering' has been happening for well over a century now. Less well-known, perhaps, is the story of Portrush and its many and varied associations with The Open Championship.

It is a remarkable story and it is told here in a unique and absorbing way by my father, retired journalist Maurice McAleese. He remembers seeing some of the top players of the day in action on the Dunluce fairways in 1951.

Essentially there are three strands to his 'Open Odyssey' – as well as having a focus on what happened on and off the course in that celebrated Championship, he touches on some of the not so well-known aspects of the Royal and Ancient game in this small corner of the world. Along the way he gives an illuminating glimpse of life in Portrush in that mid-twentieth century period.

I remember fondly the tales from this time that my father told, always with a twinkle in his eye. It was a decade when Portrush bristled with top-class hotels and boarding-houses – 220 is the figure quoted in an old guide book – so there were no worries about finding accommodation for the big invasion of Open golf fans. The course itself did not require to be altered in any substantial way – the only problem in this regard was rabbits! Their numbers were causing concern, so much so that at one stage Club members were asked to lend a hand in getting rid of them before the advent of The Open.

In his much acclaimed book, *Golf Courses of the British Isles*, published in the early part of the last century, renowned golf writer Bernard Darwin, who reported on the 1951 Open for *The Times*, describes links golf as "the exhilaration that is born of sea and sand-hills."

That kind of exhilaration is to be found in abundance on the bracing links of Royal Portrush and its "fairways of delight." Within these pages you will get a strong sense of that exhilaration. And, hopefully, some of the delight as well!

My father is a Portrush man through and through. His love of the place where he grew up and fondness for the game of golf is something I'm pleased and proud to have inherited. In neither case can I claim to match his local credentials or talent for prose. But I remain in awe of the town, the game and the author.

Anne Marie McAleese
BBC Radio Ulster

INTRODUCTION
SONG OF THE OPEN ROAD

E VEN IF YOU ARE someone who doesn't know very much about golf, you will not be too long in or about the precincts of Royal Portrush before you realise that here is a place proud of its links to what is generally recognised as the greatest Major golf tournament in the world.

For example, when I called at the Clubhouse recently I parked inadvertently in the space now permanently reserved for Darren Clarke. It has a marker shaped like a Causeway stone and bears the carved inscription "Reserved for 2011 Open Champion." How could I have missed it? I'm sure Darren Clarke would not have minded too much even if he had been coming down to the Club that day. Discreetly I moved to the adjoining space before anyone noticed.

Just across from the car park is the professionals' shop and at the entrance is a life-size poster of the smiling champion himself, holding the celebrated trophy that had eluded him for so long. In winning it he achieved an Open record for the player with most appearances (nineteen) before eventually claiming the title.

If, like me, you miss some of the clues on the way to the Clubhouse, inside you will be confronted with some that are really hard to overlook. In the spacious hallway are display cabinets filled with impressive memorabilia that sing out to you of past Open glories, including programmes from the 1951 Championship and much else besides.

In one of the cabinets you will see a beautiful replica of the Claret Jug presented to the Club by Darren Clarke to commemorate his 2011 victory, together with his gold Championship medal which he also gave into the Club's safe keeping. Both are displayed alongside Fred Daly's gold medal from 1947 when he made golfing history by becoming the first Irishman to win the Championship. Even the cabinet in which they are now housed has a link with the home of golf – it was unveiled by M Pierre Bechman, Captain of the Royal and Ancient Golf Club of St Andrews in May, 2013.

As a winner of The Open Championship, Darren Clarke has now been joined by Holywood's Rory McIlroy who also has his name carved with pride on The Open's Claret Jug and it is surely just a matter of time before Graeme McDowell joins them. He won the US Open Championship in 2010 and Rory was victorious the following year. These three players, all Major championship winners, make a formidable trio on the world golf stage and are fine ambassadors for Northern Ireland both on and off the golf course.

In 2007 Padraig Harrington became the first Irishman to win The Open Championship since Fred Daly's triumph in 1947, so in the annals of Open history he now has this enduring link with Portrush. The first player from the Republic of Ireland to win the title, he makes no secret of the fact that Royal Portrush is one of his favourite courses. He successfully defended his Open title the following year.

A replica of Graeme McDowell's US Open trophy can be seen in the nearby Rathmore Club (Royal Portrush is the parent club), and Rory's claim to fame on the Dunluce links is his stunning and record-breaking round of 61 when competing in the 2005 North of Ireland Amateur Championship. He was just 16 years old at the time. His card can be viewed in one of the Club's display cabinets. For good measure there is also a photograph of him holding the US Open trophy.

ECHOES OF OPEN HISTORY

There are still more echoes of the Royal and Ancient game's Open history as it has unfolded and impacted not only on this famous Club but also the seaside town of Portrush down through the years. I especially liked the small bronze bust of Fred Daly, enclosed in a glass display case. On a wall close by is a fine portrait of Daly, painted in oils when he was older and a more venerable figure, clutching what could be a one-iron, and still looking every inch a champion. It reminded me of what the American golfer Sam Snead said of him: "From 220 yards he could knock your hat off with a one-iron!"

You will discover also another fine portrait, this one of the legendary 'Old' Tom Morris and he takes you back to the very beginnings of golf in this part of the country. He won four Open Championships in the very early years and some time later came to Portrush to help with the design and layout of the original Dunluce links course. The portrait was presented to the Club by the Royal and Ancient Golf Club of St Andrews in 1984.

HUMBLE BEGINNINGS

In the latter part of the nineteenth century the establishment of a golf club and a modest nine-hole course, was seen as the beginning of a new era in the thriving seaside resort of Portrush. It turned out that way because, by the early 1900s, the town already had a reputation for its fine golf links, on top of its many other attractions.

It was a humble beginning but growth followed rapidly. The County Club came into being in 1888 and for the first year the game was played on a not too challenging nine-hole course. Within a year, however, the course had been extended to 18 holes. Such a good job had been made of it that within another few years, in 1895, the first professional golf tournament to be held in Ireland took place here. Incidentally this was the same year that The County Club acquired a new status and a new name; under the patronage of the Prince of Wales it was now known as The Royal Portrush Golf Club.

So the year 1895 was memorable in the golf history of Portrush. That initial professional tournament was won by the Club's first professional, Sandy Herd, who defeated a young player called Harry Vardon in the final. Both these players would go on to win The Open, Vardon on several occasions. It was in that same year also that the Club hosted the British Ladies Championship, the winner being Lady Margaret Scott, one of the most dominant figures in ladies golf at the time.

A man of renowned golfing acclaim whose association with Royal Portrush enhances still further its Open credentials is the famous golf course architect, HS (Harry) Colt, who was responsible for re-designing the Dunluce links between 1929 and 1932 and who later looked upon the finished lay-out as his greatest achievement. That really was notable because since the early part of the last century, The Open Championship has been played on a Colt designed course no fewer than forty-seven times. The story of his Portrush connection is told in an extended caption underneath his portrait which hangs in the Clubhouse.

CORRIDORS OF HISTORY

One of the walls in an upstairs corridor is filled with a splendid collection of framed photographs charting, to a large extent, the origins of the game and its historic links with Portrush. Along with photographs of Lady Margaret Scott you will find one of Joyce Wethered, another dominant figure from that

13

era. She won the title when it was played again at Royal Portrush in 1924. A finely executed drawing of Joyce Wethered, showing her in full swing, is displayed in the Royal Portrush ladies' Clubhouse. She was honoured with life membership of the Club.

From the archives, two other ladies, both members of Royal Portrush, grab your attention. To set the scene here is a short extract from the Club's annual meeting in 1900:

> "Last year the two ladies' Open Championship trophies were won by a member of the Club, and an oil portrait of the winner, Miss May Hezlet, now adorns the ladies' clubhouse. The Council have again the pleasure to record that both trophies have been retained at Portrush for another year. Miss Rhona Adair, the plucky young member by whom this distinction has been acquired, first won the Irish Championship at Portrush, and then entered the lists for The Open Championship at Westward Ho where, by her brilliant play, she won the Blue Ribbon of ladies' golf from perhaps the strongest muster of players ever seen at a ladies' competition."

Currently another young lady from Northern Ireland, also a member of Royal Portrush, which she joined in 2002 when she was just ten years old, is beginning to make her mark in the highly competitive world of Major golf. Twenty-two year old Stephanie Meadow made a magnificent debut into the professional ranks, claiming third place in the 2014 US Women's Open at Pinehurst, North Carolina. A former British Amateur Champion, she is now based in America.

So whether you are aware of it or not, the stamp of Open greatness hangs in the air and atmosphere of this place. What I have tried to do in the following pages is to convey a flavour of this while focusing mainly on the 1951 Open Championship which I am just old enough to remember. Along the way I have also tried to convey an impression of life and times in mid-twentieth century Portrush where I was born and grew up. Occasionally I have allowed myself to go down pathways I had not intended to, where I have dallied for a while and found the experience enriching, enlightening and enjoyable. As you read on, I hope you will experience some of that too.

CHAPTER 1
COUNTDOWN TO OPEN HISTORY

It would mean breaking with an old tradition

ONE OF THE MOST significant dates in the history of golf in Portrush, and in the history of The Open Championship is 14 November 1949. At a meeting on that date, the Championship Committee of the Royal and Ancient Golf Club of St Andrews, The Open's governing body, made a ground-breaking decision.

At the top of the agenda was the selection of a venue for the staging of the Championship in 1951. One of four Major championships in the world golfing calendar, in the ordinary course of events, it would probably have been a straightforward enough decision – a seaside links course somewhere on the mainland, more than likely one where the Championship would have been played before, in keeping with a long-standing tradition.

On this occasion, however, the Committee was thinking along different lines and if all went according to plan, it would mean a break with this old tradition. That's exactly what happened. Four months earlier, at a meeting of the same Committee, a decision had been taken that a sub-committee should be appointed with a view to visiting Northern Ireland and reporting on the possibilities of holding the Open Championship at either Royal County Down or Royal Portrush.

At the meeting on 14 November it was reported that the sub-committee had visited Northern Ireland and had now put forward a recommendation that the 1951 Open Championship be held over the courses at Royal Portrush and Portstewart. The recommendation was accepted.

HISTORIC BREAKTHROUGH

In February, 1951, at a meeting of the Championship Committee, the Captain of Royal Portrush, Brigadier Martin, was co-opted onto the Committee along with three others – HF Simpson, Birkdale; RP StJ Charles, Royal Porthcawl and WMB Burridge.

So the stage was finally set for the 80th Open Championship to come to Portrush. It was indeed an historic breakthrough and it would be particularly memorable for Englishman Max Faulkner. He battled through wind and rain to win his only Major title, finishing two strokes ahead of Antonio Cerda of Argentina.

In the official programme for the 1951 Open, some of the long and distinguished history as to its origin and roots in Scotland was set out. It all began in the year 1856 when, at the October meeting of the Prestwick Golf Club, it was decided to "entertain a proposition" to initiate a golf tournament for Scotland.

The idea met with general approval and was supported by most of the clubs in Scotland. However, it did not get off the ground. It was explained in the programme:

> "Whether the management of the competition proved more difficult than was anticipated, or whether the responsible Committee was somewhat apathetic, is not clear, but the project fell through and it was left to the Prestwick Club to proceed independently."

THE FIRST CHAMPIONSHIP

After drawing up a set of rules, the first competition was held at the Prestwick Club on 17 October 1860. There were eight competitors and the winner was William Park of Musselburgh who completed three rounds (then 36 holes) in 174 strokes, followed by Tom Morris, Prestwick, on 176 strokes.

Over the next half century or so the scope of the Championship was widened to include more clubs and venues and in 1951, for the first time, Royal Portrush was added to the list.

It was in 1919 that the Championship Committee of the Royal and Ancient Golf Club of St Andrews was formed specifically to look after the management of the Championship and custody of the Cup. That remained the case until 2004 when a body independent of the St Andrew's Club, known simply as the R and A was set up to administer the Championship.

The R and A kindly let me have a copy of an extract from the minutes of those relevant Championship Committee meetings dating back to 1949.

I made the approach because I wanted to know the precise timeline in the process leading up to the history-making decision to stage The Open in Portrush in 1951.

Naturally, there was a great sense of pride in the town that such a prestigious golfing event was to be played on the local links. In the official programme, this was referred to in a message by the resort's first citizen, Council chairman, Mr WR Knox. He wrote:

> "We are deeply conscious of the honour which has been done to this health and holiday resort by the selection of Royal Portrush as the venue for this Championship. It is the first time in the history of golf that The Open Championship has been played in Ireland."

A MEMORABLE VISIT

With perhaps one eye on the considerable boost which the Championship would give to the tourism profile of the town, the Chairman assured the competitors, their friends and the thousands of spectators that the people of Portrush "would spare no effort to make their stay a happy one." The beautiful surroundings and its many amenities would combine to make the visit memorable, he concluded.

In the programme foreword, Brigadier Martin, Captain of the Royal Portrush Club, said he was quite certain that every golfer in the North of Ireland would wish to join in the warm welcome the Club extended to everyone as host to The Open Championship. He hoped competitors and spectators alike would carry away nothing but happy memories.

The fact that Portstewart Golf Club, with its first-class facilities and excellent course, was within a stone's throw of Portrush, no doubt played a big factor in the decision to bring the Championship to this part of the world. This was acknowledged in the 1951 programme which also contained a message of welcome by the Captain of the Portstewart Club, Mr AE Martin. His message began:

> "We congratulate our neighbour and friendly rival, Royal Portrush Golf Club, on their initiative and successful efforts in securing the British Open Golf Championship with Portstewart as the qualifying course".

They were delighted, he continued, to share in the staging of this major event in the golfing calendar, particularly in this Festival of Britain year and on the first occasion it has been held outside Great Britain.

The prospect of The Open qualifying rounds being played on the Portstewart course had meant some disruption for the local members. In his message, the Captain explained that planned extensions and alterations to the course, which had got under way some time earlier, had to be temporarily abandoned because it would not have been possible to complete the work in time to accommodate The Open players. He added:

> "We can assure Royal Portrush of all possible assistance to make the event a success, not only during the qualifying rounds, but also for the whole meeting."

It's good to acknowledge that Portstewart played such a positive and supporting role back in 1951 and was able to bask, quite rightly so, in its own special moments of Open glory!

CHAPTER 2
OLD REMEMBERED HILLS

Bright-haired girls flitted from knoll to knoll to watch the play

THE ORIGINS OF GOLF in this part of the world, and Portrush in particular, came very much under the spotlight when it was announced that this small seaside town had been chosen as the venue for the 1951 Open Championship. It was an opportunity for journalists and others to shed some historical light on the subject and much was subsequently written in both national and international periodicals and newspapers.

Being a journalist myself (although not at the time) I thought that I might be excused if I now take a few strides of my own down some of those old, remembered fairways and if I should happen to end up in the rough in one or two places along the way I hope you will forgive me!

Don't be alarmed. I'm not going to delve too seriously or deeply because, like the famous American comedian, Jack Benny, I want to keep a light touch. He once said: "Give me golf clubs, fresh air and a beautiful partner and you can keep the clubs and the fresh air." So I was delighted to come across a humorous little sketch in one of the local newspapers from May 1888 when the game was played for the first time at Portrush following the opening of the County Club as it was then.

I found it in the archives of the *Coleraine Chronicle* and this is an extract:

"On Saturday the 'Brighton of Ireland' was disturbed to its inner centre by the inauguration of this fascinating game. Bright-haired girls – perhaps the Kitty of Coleraine among them – flitted from knoll to knoll to watch the play; and wild were the efforts of the younger players to shine in their eyes. But if you TOP your ball, and send it only three yards, under the gaze of those eyes, nothing but an earthquake can cover your confusion."

PUZZLED NATIVES

The newspaper goes on to record a further amusing colloquy among the natives who were equally puzzled and confused:

> "Eh, mon, it's a queer game this. D'ye see yon mon wi' the red coat? They tell me he's yin o' them colonels. He tuk a lang stick, an' gied the ball a crack, an' it gaed awa an' awa, till the sight o it left ma eyes. An' then he went to look for it, an' when he fund it he stoopit doon an' lookit at it for a while, an' then he walked roon an' roon it, an' then he turned his back an' walked awa frae it, an' then he came back an' tuk anither stick an' gied it a bigger whack. But it didna go anywhere; it just stuck in the sand, and he said ..."

A big contingent of golfers from the Royal Belfast Club travelled to Portrush to help launch the game on that historic day in May. Some forty players took part in the inaugural competition for a number of scratch and handicap prizes. The scratch prize was a valuable silver cup presented by the Captain of the County Club, Mr JS Alexander. Eventually, after some exciting play, the winner of the scratch prize by one stroke was a gentleman identified simply as Mr Henry while Mr Robert Kelly was the winner of the handicap prize.

The opening competition was hailed as a great success and Portrush, it was concluded, had now added a source of healthful amusement to its many attractions of scenery and sea, "which must bring a greatly increased number of visitors to the town".

A couple of decades or so later, in the summer of 1910, an unexpected visitor arrived in Portrush – Herbert Asquith, who was Prime Minister at the time. It was not an official visit – he simply wanted to play a round of golf on the now famous Dunluce links. Although his arrival was unannounced, it was nevertheless spectacular. He was on board the splendid Admiralty vessel, *Enchantress*, and accompanying him was the Chief Lord of the Admiralty, who was also apparently a keen golfer. They had brought their wives along and by all accounts enjoyed their round, stopping for tea in the Clubhouse afterwards.

The full story of the Prime Minister who paid a surprise visit to Portrush for a game of golf is told in my *Golden Strands* book so this is just a short extract describing how he made his departure from Portrush on that occasion:

"...the Prime Minister and his party decided to walk from the Clubhouse to the harbour, a comparatively short distance because in those days the Clubhouse was located at Dunluce Avenue, and hence we have the Prime Minister, with golf bag slung over his shoulder, setting off in the direction of the harbour where a small crowd had gathered. Shortly after five o'clock, two small boats were rowed out to the Enchantress and soon afterwards she slipped away as quietly as she had arrived, steaming eastward."

REMARKABLE GROWTH

At about the same time as Prime Minister Asquith's visit, a newspaper article noted that some two decades after the first golf course had been laid out on our northern coast "we have no parallel to the remarkable growth in popularity of this fascinating and healthful pastime in our midst".

The success of the Portrush Club, it was avowed, was:

"as striking as it is unprecedented in this part of the Kingdom. A similar remark may be applied to golf generally in Ulster, for there is now a chain of clubs all along our northern coast, and there are also several inland courses".

Already the neighbouring Portstewart Club had two courses, one of them of 18 holes and farther round the coast the Castlerock links had just been greatly extended. A new course had been opened at Toome. "Now wherever we look there are facilities for gratifying the popular love of golf. We may regard it as by far the most popular of out-door pastimes," was the concluding sentence in that old report.

In 1892, under the patronage of the Duke of York, the County Club became known as 'The Royal County Club' and its present name, under the patronage of the Prince of Wales, dates back to 1895.

As far as the golfing history of Portrush is concerned, it seems to have been a case of 'ladies first'. This fact was highlighted in a book by Bernard Darwin published in 1910 entitled, *The Golf Courses of the British Isles*. This renowned writer observed that Portrush had many claims to fame "and amongst others is that of having produced a wonderful race of lady golfers". He continues:

"Considering how keen they are, and how good are the courses on which they play, the men of Ireland, albeit there have been some fine players amongst them, have not so far particularly distinguished themselves, but as regards ladies golf, Ireland was for a time supreme".

A DELIGHTFUL PLACE

Two ladies in particular were singled out for mention – Miss Rhona Adair and Miss May Hezlet, both of whom used to win the championship (Irish) "one after the other with monotonous regularity, and close on their heels flocked further and innumerable members of the Hezlet family".

There was speculation as to whether there might be some 'subtle qualities' about the course which naturally tended to the development of female champions. If that was the case, Mr Darwin had not discovered them. His conclusion was that Portrush was a delightful place to play golf "for persons of either sex".

Right from the start, in Portrush at any rate, golf seems to have held a fascinating attraction for ladies for whatever reason. At the club's first monthly competition in June, 1888, for example, the *Coleraine Chronicle* reported:

"A large number of onlookers, among whom were many ladies, followed the several couples around the course, and seemed greatly interested in the fortunes and misfortunes of the various aspirants to golfing fame. One or two ladies in particular were so enthusiastic as to go four rounds, equivalent to a walk of nearly eight miles".

The ladies crop up again in another piece of reportage flagging up some of the "domestic virtues" of the game:

"With the salt-delicious air from the sea around him, and the wild thyme sending up its odour as he walks, the golfer breathes an atmosphere of health and joy, his only terror the bunker, his worst troubles a bad lie, a broken club, a topped ball.

"Nor is he denied, if he desires it, the society of the gentler sex, some of whom wield the cleek with skill and grace. Others indeed display more ankle than skill; but that is a passing stage. Some of the clubs have strange, suggestive names – the 'Long Spoon', the 'Short Spoon', the 'Masher!' Can this be mere accident? Is it not rather a touch of prophetic insight, looking on to a day, already arrived in

Scotland, when women shall have invaded the sacred precincts of the links and broken into the selfish foursome.

"Golf cultivates the domestic virtues too, though one has heard a golfer's wife speak severely of the rival goddess. On Friday evening at Portrush, almost in the gloaming, two ladies played an interesting and breathless 'single' and it was a touching and beautiful thing to see the meek devotion of the attendant husbands, who kept the score and carried the clubs."

AN OUTLET FOR SUPERFLUOUS ENERGY

An explanation as to why so many women were taking up the game was given in 1904 by a Portrush golfing super-star, May Hezlet, who won many competitions at national and local level, including the Irish and British Open Championships. She wrote:

"It is now generally acknowledged that golf is the game – par excellence – for women. The girl of the present day must have some outlet for her superfluous energy, and she is not content with the life which women were expected to lead in former years.

"In those days their principal occupations were household duties, and sewing or embroidery. Exercise was not considered needful, and a quiet walk in the garden was the only change permitted from the work-chamber or still room. Household duties are a very necessary part of life, and sewing and amusements of the like nature are excellent in moderation, but they are not enough to satisfy the tastes of the modern girl. Exercise in the open air is a necessity to her, and when combined with healthful bodily exertion, so much the better."

The appeal of the game in Portrush in those early days would seem to have been magnetic as yet another piece of local reporting tends to confirm:

"The air is so fine that the temptation to play three rounds is very hard to overcome, while I may quote (solely on the authority of a friend), this further testimonial to it, that it has the unique property of enabling one to drink a bottle of champagne every night and feel the better for it."

Perhaps that was going a bit too far. In more recent times, however, champagne corks have been popping thanks to the likes of Fred Daly, Darren Clarke and Graeme McDowell. Fred Daly is from a different era, of course, but Clarke and McDowell, together with Rory McIlroy, stride majestically along the fairways of world golf.

Undoubtedly the outstanding success of this formidable trio and the smooth running of the Irish Open Championship when it was played here in 2012, were big factors in persuading the R & A to bring The Open Championship back to Portrush where the fairways have been little altered since 1951 when it was staged so successfully in this 'Brighton of Ireland'.

"The Ladies' Championship at Portrush resulted in a victory for Miss Dorothy Campbell, the holder of the United States and Canadian ladies' championships and the British champion of 1909. She defeated Miss Violet Hezlet in the final by 3 up and 2 to play. It was Miss Hezlet's first appearance in a championship final and she is to be congratulated on the plucky fight she made against her redoubtable opponent."

From a report in the Northern Constitution, *May 1911*

CHAPTER 3

PETER ALLISS: A MEMORY OF 1951

Faulkner brought a touch of colour to our very dull lives

ONE OF THE YOUNGEST competitors, if not the youngest, in the 1951 Open Championship was 21-year-old Peter Alliss (Ferndown), making his debut as a professional. Today Peter Alliss is very well known as a commentator for the BBC at most of the big golf tournaments. He is also involved in other aspects of the game, notably as a course designer. Upwards of fifty golf courses have been laid out to his specification and he is also a prolific author, having produced more than a score of golf books.

When the idea occurred to me that it would be nice to have a comment from someone who actually played in that 1951 Championship, his name came to mind. And when I contacted him through his official website, he kindly obliged.

I had simply asked what memories he had of Portrush and of playing in his first Major Championship there. This was his response:

"I'd just completed two years National Service with the RAF Regiment so was very much out of practice. I was chaperoned by my brother Alec.

"I remember the large crowds, the wonderful golf course, the rather dreary weather but very formidable golf course and Max Faulkner's splendid victory. It was quite a good time for British players – Fred Daly had won the Championship in 1947 and Henry Cotton in 1948. In 1949 and 1950 it went to Bobby Locke of South Africa, and then in 1951 it was the turn of Max Faulkner. He was a very flamboyant character who brought a touch of colour to our very dull lives.

"I'm delighted at the possibility that the Championship could return there over the next few years. It's certainly a wonderful setting, well worthy of a Championship. Good luck with your book.

Peter Alliss"

A nice reflection there from Peter Alliss and no doubt he was delighted with the announcement shortly afterwards that the Championship would be returning to Portrush in 2019. I've heard him refer to the Royal Portrush links sometimes during the course of his commentaries at the Major Championships and always in a complimentary manner. And although he says he was "out of practice" when he came to Portrush in 1951, he showed flashes of the skill and brilliance with which his career would later be marked, equalling the course record of 69 in one of the qualifying rounds.

It had been a record-breaking day. This is taken from a *Belfast Telegraph* report:

> "In one crowded half-hour of glorious golf at Portrush, the record of 69 set up on Monday by Arthur Lees (Sunningdale) was equalled by the tall, 21-year-old Peter Alliss (Ferndown) and then twice broken, first by Bobby Locke with an immaculate 67 and next by Jack Hargreaves (Sutton Coldfield) with a tremendous 66."

Just a couple of years later, Peter Alliss had good reason to remember his clash with Fred Daly when they met in the third round of the British Matchplay Championship. Fred had been drawn in the second round against Alan 'Tiger' Poulson and after 18 holes the match was all square. So it was a case of sudden death tie holes and finally, after just over five hours on the course, Fred won at the 12th tie hole.

That clash set a record for the longest match but the day's play was not yet over. After just a ten minute break, he then played "an up and coming professional" called Peter Alliss in the third round and far from showing signs of exhaustion, produced scintillating golf, beating the younger player by 6 and 5 in the space of one hour and fifty minutes.

It gives a glimpse of some of the skill, stamina and dogged determination with which Fred Daly was endowed and which played a big part throughout his glittering career.

CHAPTER 4
CUTTING A DASH ON THE COURSE

For his age he was reckoned to be the best player in Ireland

Portrush owes much of its appeal and development over the years to the game of golf, so 1951 can be regarded as a high water mark in its history. The tourism boost which The Open brought with it was felt throughout the whole of the summer and for a good many summers afterwards.

At the beginning of that century, an editorial in the local weekly newspaper, *The Northern Constitution*, had proclaimed:

> "Everyone who has studied the history of Irish golf is forced to the conclusion that the prosperity which Portrush has attained in recent years is, in a very sensible measure, due to the attractions which the Golf Club has provided for visitors since its establishment…"

It was a time when more and more people were starting to play golf. The Royal Portrush links course, even then, was acknowledged to be one of the best in the United Kingdom and for many visitors the lure of its well manicured fairways was irresistible. As that old editorial went on to highlight, many championships had been played on the course in recent years.

The reason the newspaper was drawing attention to this fact was that the Club, "with a view to providing better facilities for members and visitors", wanted to provide fourteen new holes on land stretching to the White Rocks, which had lately been acquired. Club officials were trying to negotiate a new lease for the land with Lord Antrim. "If negotiations with the Earl of Antrim conclude satisfactorily, there is a bright future in store for the Royal Portrush Club," it was predicted.

That prediction did come true and just over four decades later the Royal Portrush Club reached a pinnacle with the staging of the Open Championship over the famous Dunluce links. It was won by Max Faulkner, a very stylish English player both in technique and dress. One of the competitors on that occasion in 1951 was Fred Daly who had won the title four years earlier, in 1947, and who was a native of Portrush. On this occasion, however, he had to settle for joint fourth place.

A DISTINGUISHED MEMBER

One of the most distinguished members of Royal Portrush at the turn of the last century was Dr Anthony Traill, Provost of Trinity College, Dublin and brother of William Acheson Traill, of Causeway tram fame. Evidently Dr Traill cut quite a dash on the golf course with, as noted by a correspondent of the time, "his wide flannel trousers and aggressive looking boots, hurriedly pursuing his ball."

The same correspondent went on to tell an amusing story as to how the great man came to take up the game in the first place. One day he was standing outside the tramway depot in Portrush, waiting for a tram, when his attention was drawn to two aspiring golfers who were said to be "making desperate but ineffectual efforts to drive the famous 'Crater bunker'" – a large and steep sided bunker at the 17th fairway.

After watching them for a while Dr Traill "who does not suffer from shyness" went over to them and told them what he thought of their efforts. He was immediately challenged to have a go himself if he thought he could do any better. The story goes: "At the first attempt the Dr landed the ball on the green and departed in triumph," presumably leaving the two beginners scratching their heads in amazement. Dr Traill went on to become a very competent player and at the time when this little anecdote was being recalled (in March, 1903) he was reckoned to be "at his age" the best player in Ireland.

DOWN TO THE WIRE

From time to time a golf correspondent would be tipped off about some unusual incident which had occurred on the links and these were faithfully reported. This is how one such incident was recorded in the *Northern Constitution*:

"Golfers, more especially golfers not quite up to championship level, are occasionally surprised by the vagaries of the ball in its flight from the tee. The other day a player on the first tee at Portrush made a fine, strong swipe with his driver and the ball, swerving slightly to the right, struck one of the wire stays of the flagpole and rebounded back past the Clubhouse with such vigour that its wild career was only terminated by the long grass between the Clubhouse and Golf Terrace. Happily, no one was injured."

Interestingly, in the same notes, the names of two famous golfers were mentioned – Sandy Herd and Harry Vardon. Apparently they had been "astonishing the Donegal natives" that week by some fine play at Rosapenna. Vardon had first visited Ulster some 15 years earlier when "in a great professional tournament" at Royal Portrush he was beaten by Herd on the final hole.

It was at Royal Portrush that Herd had set out on his distinguished professional career. He had been appointed Club professional in 1890, his first professional appointment. He was recommended for the post by one of the all-time golfing greats, Tom Morris, known as the "grand old man of golf," who also had an interesting link with Royal Portrush, having helped with the lay-out and design of the course.

In that old tournament, Morris was Herd's caddie and mentor and together they were a formidable team. One report of the match mentioned the fact that Morris was not too keen on Sunday golf, recalling what he had once said to two English players on the subject: "If you twa gentlemen dinna need a rest on the Sabbath, the links does." An amusing story is also told of Morris when he met Andrew Carnegie who was in St Andrews to receive the freedom of the city. They had a long conversation and at the conclusion, Carnegie gave Tom his card, on which he had written on the back: "Tom Morris, king of golfdom, your loyal subject. AC"

THE MATCH WAS KEENLY CONTESTED

The final paragraph from another report on that professional tournament over the Portrush links gives a great insight into the character of old Tom Morris:

"Herd's match with Vardon was very keenly contested, having only been won on the last green. When the two players came to the penultimate green Herd's ball was found lying about six feet from the hole, while his opponent had played the odd and lay dead. Scarcely a word had been exchanged between Herd and Morris all the way round, but the latter now walked solemnly forward, lifted the flag, and with a stern look at Herd, said, 'Saundy, there's the hole.' Sandy did as his old master suggested and holed the putt."

In those days Vardon was something of a legend in the realms of golf, having won The Open Championship no fewer than six times. He was also the first British player to win the US Open.

Sandy Herd, a Scotsman, had won the British Open in 1902. In August of that year he was back in Portrush playing an exhibition match on the Royal Portrush links. It was reported in a leading golf magazine:

"Herd was seen at his very best. He could hardly, it seemed, do anything wrong and, in addition to great brilliance, his play was marked by marvellous consistency. His splendid total of 70 establishes a new record for the course, a record which, if I mistake not, will take a deal of beating."

A big gallery of spectators watched the match and among the crowd was another prominent golfer of the day. The same correspondent wrote:

"It is interesting to note that the most prominent lady golfer of the day was also on the Portrush links on Saturday. I allude to Miss May Hezlet, the ladies' Open champion who, it was noticed, followed the course of the play with keen interest."

Sandy Herd

CHAPTER 5

PORTRUSH IS CALLING YOU...

*The accommodation was luxurious with large public rooms
overlooking the sea*

WHEN THE OPEN CHAMPIONSHIP was being played in Portrush in the summer of 1951, the town could boast upwards of thirty hotels. Some could be classified as small, private hotels but nevertheless they offered a high standard of accommodation. Apart from hotels, the number of boarding and guest houses could be counted in the hundreds. So there were no problems with accommodation for the huge numbers of golfing enthusiasts who flocked to Portrush for The Open extravaganza.

Many of the visitors would have been able to pick up a free copy of the official Portrush Guide which contained a mine of information about many of the establishments and gave a comprehensive outline of just what was available to the holidaymaker apart altogether from the golf.

Some of the larger hotels were almost like miniature holiday camps. For instance, one of the best known was the Skerry-Bhan on Lansdowne Crescent "ideally situated facing the Atlantic." An advertisement in the Guide drew attention to the fact that it had distant views of the East Strand, White Rocks, Dunluce Castle and the Giant's Causeway.

The hotel was also close to tennis, bowling, and a putting green at the Recreation Grounds and a bathing pool (the Blue Pool) was only three minutes away. The famous championship golf course was only fifteen minutes away.

The accommodation was luxurious with large public rooms overlooking the sea, sun lounge and ballroom with maple floor, large panelled dining-room seating 130, well appointed bedrooms with hot and cold running water and, it was emphasised, an electric lift to all floors.

The most famous hotel, the Northern Counties, was also featured in the Guide. It was close to the Royal Portrush links, had 150 bedrooms (many with own bathroom), the finest ballroom in Ireland, hot and cold sea-water baths, and a tennis court. There was also a heated sea-water swimming pool. Although it was not mentioned in the advertisement, the pool was open throughout the winter months and used a lot by locals, including myself, and it was always an enjoyable experience.

For a period during the war years this hotel had been occupied for use as a school by Campbell College and had resumed normal service on 1 July 1946. It was reported that "bookings are considerable." Earlier that year it was noted in a news report:

> "During recent months the hotel has been in the hands of contractors who are putting the finishing touches to an elaborate scheme of general renewal. Special attention has been given to redecoration and furnishings, the resultant effect imparting a pleasing impression of familiar surroundings decked out in bright new garb. All the old amenities have been restored, including the popular salt-water swimming pool."

The hotel was then still owned by the LMS NCC railway and at the opening ceremony, Lord Massereene, of the railway company, said they were leaving nothing undone to make the hotel as attractive and popular as it had always been in the days before the war.

AN OPEN FORECAST

Speaking on behalf of Royal Portrush Golf Club, Lord Justice Babington congratulated the company on the transformation and referred to the important role played by the hotel in attracting tourists and others to Portrush. He also highlighted the friendly relations between the railway company and the Golf Club, adding: "We look forward to housing the British Amateur and Open Championships in the not too distant future in Portrush, in which connection the hotel will be a valuable asset."

Another speaker, Colonel CO Hezlet, envisaged also in the near future growing numbers of golfers flying from London and elsewhere across the water for golfing weekends in Portrush.

Also worthy of mention is Fawcett's Royal Portrush Hotel situated close to the Northern Counties. It specialised in conducted tours and throughout the summer bus parties arrived from all parts of the United Kingdom. The hotel also had a ballroom, central heating, an electric lift and a resident orchestra.

Alas, all three of those splendid hotels no longer exist. The Northern

Counties was destroyed by fire in the 1990s and the site was redeveloped and includes another hotel, the Ramada. The Skerry-Bhan and Fawcett's disappeared in the course of re-development schemes.

The man in charge of sorting out holiday accommodation in Portrush at this time was Captain WR Shutt, a larger than life character and a very genial gentleman whose personality was as large as his stature. I got to know him well when I was a cub reporter gathering news items for the Portrush Notes column of the *Coleraine Chronicle*. I would call with him and many others, including clergymen, who had their finger on what was happening in and around the town. Captain Shutt had his office at the spacious Recreation Grounds at the top of the town and I rarely came away without an interesting morsel of news for that week's paper.

BOOKING SERVICE

A letter in the official Guide written by Captain Shutt gives a 'how times have changed' insight into booking a holiday by the seaside five or six decades ago.

"Dear Sir or Madam," he started off, "The Bureau will be pleased to help you and your friends to secure accommodation. If you would like to use this service, complete the form on the back hereof, and return same with a cheque or postal order for 2/6 to cover cost of postage, printing, etc".

How it worked was that particulars of the accommodation required would be passed on to establishments able to meet the requirements "and you may expect to receive one or two direct offers from which to select". It was then up to the clients to get in touch directly with the establishment that suited. All those advertised in the Guide had been registered with the Northern Ireland Tourist Board and the Holiday Information Bureau.

The form at the back of the letter was simple. Questions to be answered included ages of children (if any), number of bedrooms required, number of beds in each room and whether full board, bed and breakfast or apartments only would be required. There was also space to state the situation of the hotel or boarding house preferred and to help with this the Guide contained a pull-out street map of the town. To be filled in also was the date and hour of arrival, date and hour of departure, whether or not a licensed hotel was required and the "approximate amount you desire to pay per person per week". Prospective visitors using this form of booking were urged to "give full details". I wonder how much it was used. It would be interesting to have sight of one of those old forms filled in and giving full details!

One of the many boarding and guest houses featured in the advertising space in that particular Guide book was my mother's establishment in Causeway Street, 'Kerrville', situated "one minute to sands," under personal supervision and providing "excellent cuisine". Alas, I cannot say whether or not my mother received many, if any, bookings resulting from her little display but I can vouch for the excellent cuisine and do know that there were always plenty of guests, many of them coming from Belfast, Glasgow and many other places summer after summer.

A NICE PLACE TO LIVE

There is a nice little profile of life in Portrush in those old days in a section of the Guide entitled "Why not live there?" It states:

"Portrush has its winter residential attractiveness little less than its summer. Houses, both furnished and unfurnished, are usually available at moderate rents. To town dwellers the low rates seem even a commendable item, while coal, gas and electricity are also on the same economic scale.

"The population, which rises to 14,000 or more in summer, is normally about 4,000. The social side of life is well cared for with six libraries and a newsroom, and with shops which provide the latest books and London daily newspapers etc".

The charms and delights of Portrush in winter were considerable with musical, dramatic and literary entertainments helping to pass the evenings. For anyone who liked hunting, the Meets of the nearby Route Harriers were a big attraction. In the concluding words of that old Guide:

"...Portrush is calling you to a renewed inspiration and a brighter outlook as well as to a re-invigoration of mind and body, amongst such scenery and charms that you will recall them year after year".

Having grown up in Portrush in that wonderful era, I can only say amen to that!

CHAPTER 6
A GREAT FESTIVAL FOR ALL

The town took on a carnival atmosphere

THE WEEK BEFORE THE Open teed off at Royal Portrush in 1951, an
ambitious programme of events got under way as part of the town's
Festival of Britain contribution.

The Festival of Britain was a national exhibition organised by the
Government to help give the country a lift in the aftermath of the war and to
highlight Britain's contribution to science, technology and the arts. Towns
and villages up and down the country organised their own programme of
Festival events.

In Portrush the Festival got off to a good start with a religious service on
Ramore Hill on the Sunday and throughout the week there was a packed
programme of entertainment for visitors and residents alike. A report in the
Coleraine Chronicle noted:

> "The aim was to provide both indoor and outdoor attractions of a
> varied character and the organisers had the assistance of people
> interested in the show and entertainment business."

The town took on a carnival atmosphere, the main street brilliantly
illuminated each night with coloured fairy lights as well as flags and bunting.

That service on Ramore Hill attracted a huge attendance, some 2,500
people on its green slopes. Before the service there had been a parade
through the town, headed by Portrush Pipe Band, in which all the leading
local organisations were represented.

Throughout the week events included a display at the harbour by the
crew of Portrush lifeboat, a demonstration of fire-fighting and rescue work
at Lansdowne Crescent and the finals of various games competitions at the
Recreation Grounds.

There was a touch of glamour, too, because many of the Festival events
were graced by the presence of three local girls who had been successful in

the final of a lengthy series of weekly heats of the 'Miss Festival of Britain' beauty contest held in Barry's Ballroom. The three who finally won through were Miss Nan McAleese, Miss Jeanene McCandless and Miss Betty Meekin. Yes, Nan was my sister and I well remember that happy time and the pride and joy of family and friends.

I mentioned that the Festival of Britain beauty heats were held in Barry's Ballroom. It was part of the Barry's Amusements complex, a major centre of entertainment in Portrush as it still is today, although the ballroom is no more.

In July of that year the ballroom played host to The Harold Smart Quartet, a combination hailed at the time as 'Britain's best quartet', having been featured in many of the BBC's top entertainment programmes, including *Rainbow Room*, *Sing it Again* and *Music While You Work*. They had also, it was noted in a press release, "made gramophone recordings."

VARIETY RAINBOW

Barry's also contributed to the Portrush summer programme of events in other ways and that summer their Variety Rainbow promotion in the Town Hall attracted capacity audiences. It had an all-star cast, including Conne Stewart, billed as Ireland's top television star; Larry Peters "the amazing voice of Al Jolson", Helen Carter, child entertainer of stage, screen and radio; Joe Devoe, Europe's greatest juggler; Leslie Mann, sentimental gentleman of song; Joan Willis, talented pianist; Leila Webster, from Belfast Hippodrome.

It was announced that the show would be changed each week and in addition it was proposed to introduce top-line guest artists from England.

In those days Portrush had a Minstrel Troupe and at the show they produced for the Festival there was a special guest in the audience, none other than the great Bobby Locke from South Africa who was defending his Open Championship title, having won it for the previous two years.

A top celebrity visitor to Portrush at about the same time was the distinguished broadcaster, Richard Dimbleby, presenter of the popular BBC programme, *Down Your Way*. He had come to Portrush to record an edition of the programme. He interviewed a number of prominent local people and the programme was broadcast later. The interviewees had to select their favourite piece of music. That programme would be worth listening to again, I'm sure, because it would give a revealing insight into what life was like in Portrush in that historic mid-twentieth century period. The Open is returning to Portrush so perhaps the BBC might be persuaded to air that edition of *Down Your Way* again.

Another VIP visitor to Portrush arrived just too late for The Open but he probably was not unduly worried because it was not on his itinerary anyway. The Kabaka of Buganda, Edward Muteesa, stopped at Portrush during a four-day visit to Northern Ireland. He travelled via the Antrim Coast and he and his wife and others in the party were entertained to tea by the local Council.

IMPRESSING THE KABAKA

A press report of his visit states: "The Kabaka, who is 26, is an independent ruler in direct treaty relations with the Imperial Government by virtue of the Uganda Agreement of 1900 and is one of the most important Grenadier Guards."

He stayed overnight in the Northern Counties Hotel and was, apparently, particularly impressed with the hotel's indoor swimming pool.

Meanwhile, plans for The Open were reaching a climax as a report in the *Coleraine Chronicle* highlighted:

> "The stage is now set for the battle between the cream of the world's professional and amateur golfers for The Open Championship over the testing Portrush and Portstewart links next week. Latest reports are that everything is in readiness for the big event, and officials are on their toes to make certain that no hitch occurs to disturb the organisation of the event."

In the weeks and months leading up to the Championship there had been some voices of gloom and doom predicting that The Open would not be a success at Portrush. Interviewed afterwards, Commander JA Storer-Carson, secretary of the Royal and Ancient, told a reporter:

> "The arrangements were excellent; nothing was left undone. The greens, tees and fairways were perfect and the crowd control was first-class."

The Commander added that never in all his experience had he seen such well behaved galleries. He estimated that the total attendance was between 10,000 and 12,000, with about 6,000 to 7,000 watching the final day's play.

According to a correspondent in one of the local newspapers, "golf fever" was in the air on the final day of the tournament "and a hustle to the links was evident morning and afternoon."

THE WIND DOTH BLOW

A leading golf correspondent of the day, Frank Pennink, wrote:

> "I hope they play The Open at Portrush again. I think it is just about the finest course we have in these islands and so did most of the contestants."

Another sports writer summed it up this way:

> "The Portrush course was a great test once the Championship got into its stride. For the first three days it deceived competitors by playing easily but when the wind got up it provided a stiff test even for the best golfers."

One player who coped very well with the windy conditions was the eventual winner, Max Faulkner. There was only a suggestion of a breeze to fan the sweltering galleries as the first round was played on Wednesday. From then on it was entirely different. A strong wind blew and veered tantalisingly making conditions difficult for the players.

Described in a press report as "the glamour boy of the greens," Faulkner did a couple of handsprings on the last green following his final putt. With that flamboyant gesture he put the finishing touch to a round of golf which ensured that he would always have a unique place in the annals of The Open Championship history.

First tee and 18th Green

CHAPTER 7

FAIRWAYS OF DELIGHT

Hotel guests could play on the Dunluce links free of charge

THE FORTUNES OF PORTRUSH were given a boost in the latter part of the nineteenth century when golf came to its shores. According to a news report in the *Northern Whig* in May 1888, however, Portrush was already "pre-eminent in Ireland as a first-class watering place."

The *Whig*, a daily newspaper published in Belfast, which closed a good many years ago, continued:

> "Year by year, owing to the enterprise of the inhabitants and the watchful attention of the Belfast and Northern Counties Railway Company, Portrush has enhanced its reputation… and now that the facilities for reaching the Causeway have been brought as close as possible to perfection, that favourite haunt of the tourist, health-seeker and naturalist has come to be patronised in a measure commensurate with its world-wide celebrity."

A few years earlier, the Giant's Causeway and Bushmills Hydro-electric Tramway, which ran between Portrush and the Causeway, had been inaugurated. At the time, Portrush was not just catering for the needs of tourists. The needs of the inhabitants were not being overlooked. Work was proceeding apace on the construction of a large number of houses "fitted with all recent improvements and conveniences." The more affluent residents were "determined that complaints of insufficient house accommodation shall henceforth be groundless."

The *Whig* report also noted that "convincing proofs of the activity of the Improvement Committee are everywhere apparent". The princely sum of £140 had been spent on general repairs "to the public advantage."

Turning to hotel accommodation, the writer found that they were fully equipped and some had been enlarged and renovated. The "palatial" Northern

Counties Hotel was singled out for special mention; in recent months its public baths had been greatly enlarged and improved.

That hotel had a special link with the new County Golf Club and guests had the privilege of playing a round of golf on the Dunluce links course free of charge.

At the Golf Hotel, overlooking the West Bay beach, several new bedrooms had been added and a new billiard room opened on the ground floor, its former location on the second floor having been converted into a reading and writing room. A *Coleraine Chronicle* report from the same time stated:

> "A fair number of houses have been let for June, and already indications of the coming stir and bustle are to be seen in the streets."

In the same newspaper, an article entitled "A Spring Visit to the Seaside" began with the observation that visitors to Portrush would find that favourite resort "wholly and entirely given over to the hands of the builder and the painter."

> "Those who see the town in the months of March and April would scarcely know it again should they re-visit it in July or August. But this is not the only thing which gives the town an altered look. What a dull, almost dismal look Portrush has in the depths of winter, with the wind howling and shrieking, and driving small stones and sand into one's face!
>
> "No doubt the sea has a wildly grand appearance, the spray dashing over the Skerries and the huge waves washing their strength against the Ramore cliffs. What a change comes with the advent of summer. Houses which were unattractive and dreary become bright and inviting, and the hotels, formerly resembling castles of inanity are transformed into scenes of life and bustle, with representatives of the world of fashion present in abundance."

There was one discordant note, however, and it had to do with the fact that a band had not as yet been engaged for the season. *The Chronicle* reported:

> "As to the expediency of spending £300 or £400 on the engagement of a band there is locally much difference of opinion; but in any case instrumental music will not be altogether absent during the coming busy months, seeing that a military band from Belfast will be engaged to play at Portrush once or twice a week.".

It was also noted that the three games of golf, cricket and tennis – each with a club of its own – were now flourishing in the place. There was, too, every hope that a series of diving and swimming exhibitions at the Blue Pool would be arranged on a more elaborate scale than in former years.

Fast-forward ten years to the last summer of the nineteenth century and the picture of Portrush is no less encouraging. In a "Jottings from the Seaside" feature in the same local newspaper the season was being described as one of "infinite satisfaction". It was observed: "The town is larger than ever before, and yet there is not an empty house or hotel that has not its fullest complement of visitors."

Much of the credit for this state of affairs was down to the efforts of the newly formed Portrush Advertising Committee which had produced and distributed across the channel a series of attractive posters, pictures and pamphlets extolling the virtues and attractions of this part of the Antrim coast.

Apparently the Advertising Committee had spent large sums of money "to disseminate a knowledge of the attractions of Portrush as a seaside resort." A fine pictorial poster depicting a beautiful bird's eye view of the resort and surrounding countryside, as well as a twenty-page pamphlet had been distributed to outlets in Scotland and the North of England.

Arrangements had also been made to exhibit the poster at several hundred railway stations in Scotland and it would also be posted at a number of railway stations in England and on hoardings in places such as Manchester, Leeds, Liverpool and other North of England towns.

Some details of the pamphlet were given and it seems to have contained very comprehensive information.

> "It is illustrated by a sketch map of the Antrim Coast and eight full page reproductions of photographs of Portrush and the Giant's Causeway and contains eight pages of descriptive letterpress, giving all necessary information for tourists and other visitors. Other forms of advertising have also been taken advantage of by the Committee and altogether the members have turned to excellent account the funds which have been placed at their disposal."

The popularity of Portrush as a holiday destination had a knock-on effect for the Golf Club; by now it had become the Royal Portrush Golf Club. It was reported that not for several years had the Clubhouse and links been so extensively availed of by golfers as at present. As described in the *Northern Constitution*:

"The crowds of golfers remind one of the early 'golf fever' days when a much larger proportion of members went over the course in the summer months, and low charges brought hundreds of visitors. Visitors' terms are higher now than in those days, but lower and more elastic than they were three or four years ago. The Council of the Club were not at first quite successful in the choice of a secretary but the duties are now being admirably discharged by Major Elmitt, a very energetic, clever and experienced officer."

The link between Portrush and the Giant's Causeway via the old electric trams also played a part, no doubt, in the increasing prosperity and popularity of Portrush. That same summer it was "fully expected" that the season would be a very busy one at the Giant's Causeway. According to the same newspaper:

"A pleasing activity is again visible at the two Causeway hotels, while the owners of tea and souvenir stands are giving the finishing touches to their miniature places of business.

"The commodious and neatly designed pavilion erected by the Causeway Company last season is open, and here light refreshments of all kinds may now be had, in full view of the Causeway. Since last season the excellent path constructed along the face of the magnificent eastward cliffs has been still further improved, and no visitor to the Causeway should miss this easy method of seeing the Amphitheatre and the noble cliffs and headlands in that direction."

As a young boy I well remember, on family visits to the Causeway, walking down the narrow pathway leading to the famous stones, being fascinated by the string of small wooden huts strewn all the way along. They were well stocked with souvenirs of all descriptions, many of them hand-made, and the stall-holders were friendly and knowledgeable about the history, the myth and legend, of the Causeway. Although some of the huts were a little the worse for wear, they added to the mystique and atmosphere of the place and I felt that some of this was lost when they were eventually removed.

CHAPTER 8

DELIVERING THE GOODS

A little bit of postal history was also made

IT WAS NOT ONLY golfing history that was made in Portrush in the summer of 1951. A little bit of postal history was also made.

How did that come about? It came in the shape of a mobile post office. Apparently it was the first time something like this had been used at a golf championship or indeed any other sporting event in Northern Ireland.

I don't remember seeing it myself at The Open but I'm sure it was a facility much appreciated by the large crowds of spectators who would perhaps have relished the idea of being able to buy stamps and post letters and postcards without having to leave the course. I'll bet there are many collectors who would like to get their hands on one of those old postcards, perhaps one with a few comments from the sender as to how the golf was going.

Press arrangements also came under the spotlight and the Portstewart Club, where some of the qualifying rounds were played, was not happy with their press arrangements. A month or so before the big event the club had only two additional telephone lines installed. As was pointed out in a news report:

> "Compared with Portrush, which will have 35 lines in action, two teleprinters and a mobile post-office, it does seem that the officials have a genuine grievance here. Further efforts are being made to have additional lines, and it is hoped these meet with success."

Whatever happened, whether or not Portstewart did manage to have a few more lines installed, the whole communications set-up was a far cry from the highly advanced technology in evidence today, giving massive coverage to such sporting events.

Nowadays press and media coverage of such events is on a massive scale and gives quite a boost to tourism. I came across some interesting statistics relevant to this with regard to coverage of the 1995 Senior British Open Championship played at Portrush.

They were contained in a news report in the *Coleraine Chronicle* under the headline, "Roll up, roll up for a media circus the like of which we've never seen…" The report stated:

> "A staggering 231 million homes around the globe will enjoy highlights from the fairways at Royal Portrush beamed directly into their living-rooms. This figure does not include the 95 million watching the action 'live' in the United States and the United Kingdom courtesy of SKY and ABC and a series of news items scheduled to appear on Trans World Sport, CNN International, Reuters and America's largest cable sports network, ESPN."

All of this, it was concluded, amounted to previously unequalled exposure, not just for golf and Royal Portrush, but also for the Province as a whole.

Preparations had been made for "a veritable invasion" of hacks, camera crews and television presenters from as far afield as Argentina, Japan, South Africa and Malaysia, all focussing on "a peaceful landscape punctuated only by the cries of angst-ridden golfers battling with the vagaries and delights of the Dunluce Links."

A far cry from that 1951 mobile post-office. I can't be sure but it was probably a caravan adapted for the purpose. Caravans were not too much in evidence in Portrush in those days, nevertheless, there was a caravan angle to The Open Championship.

In the *Belfast Telegraph* an advertisement for caravans posed the question: "Going to Portrush for The Open?" The answer was given in this way:

> "Wouldn't miss it – should be a real 'festival of golf'. I'm taking the family along.
> "Fixed up your hotel yet?
> "No need to. I've just bought a caravan from… Plan to park it at one of those beauty spots along the coast and see The Open at our leisure. Solves the problem of being really convenient to the course…"

I suppose it would have been possible to pick a nice spot and just park up your caravan for a day or two without much worry of being moved on. How times have changed.

By and large, press coverage of The Open was positive but afterwards one jarring note was struck. It came from Ballycastle and it concerned accommodation during the golf week – the complaint was that Ballycastle had been overlooked.

The flack was directed at the Ulster Tourist Association. At a meeting of the town council, Mr AD McAuley, a leading businessman in Ballycastle, drew attention to the fact that in the publication issued by the Association in connection with accommodation during The Open Championship, no mention had been made of Ballycastle. This was in spite of the fact that other towns "with inferior accommodation" were mentioned in detail.

A report of the council meeting in the *Coleraine Chronicle* continued: "He did not think that eighteen miles was a prohibitive distance from Portrush for those seeking accommodation during the week of the Championship".

Councillor McAuley went on to recall that a representative of the Ulster Tourist Association had visited Ballycastle in search of advertisements from hotels and boarding-house proprietors. These people, he said, paid to have advertisements inserted in Ulster Tourist Association publications and were surely entitled to a fair deal.

At that meeting it was not only the Ulster Tourist Association which came under the negative spotlight in this connection – the Ulster Transport Authority was also in the firing line. According to Councillor McAuley, repeated requests had been made for excursion fares from Ballycastle to various sporting events to be introduced but the Authority had taken no steps to provide such facilities. Neither were excursions to Ballycastle available such as were already in operation to Portrush, Bangor and other seaside resorts. He thought it was time something was done to bring Ballycastle within easy reach of the travelling public. An isolationist policy was not the aim of the Council and they were going to see that it was not forced upon them.

His proposal that the Ulster Transport Authority and the Ulster Tourist Association "be written to" with regard to these matters, was adopted unanimously.

CHAPTER 9

HOW IT ALL BEGAN

*Knowledge of the game can only be acquired by much study
and weariness of the flesh*

A FEW HELPFUL TIPS and suggestions as to how the game of golf should be played were given in an article published in the *Northern Constitution* newspaper in May 1888 to mark the beginning of a new and exciting chapter in the sporting history of Portrush. It is quoted here in full:

"A new source of interest has this season been provided at Portrush by the institution of a golf club and the introduction of that Royal and Ancient game into this part of Ulster.

The pastime is not normally associated with those in which young ladies indulge but as a recreation for those 'lords of creation' who naturally grow weary of looking at waves churning among the rocks or watching the flaming red sun dropping daily (cloudy days excepted) into the sea, the game is not to be surpassed, even in this crowded age of cricket, tennis and lacrosse etc.

The club, we understand, has been established at Portrush chiefly through the energy and thoughtfulness of Mr Bailey from Belfast and the proprietors of the Northern Counties Hotel, acting in judicious conjunction with several golfing experts who occasionally visit our favourite watering-place.

The Hotel Company have rented the breezy sand-hills to the east of the railway station and kindly given the club the free use of them. These grounds form, we believe, one of the best golfing 'links' in the Kingdom.

The County Golf Club as it has been called – though the name of the county might as well have been put into the title – is already an unquestionable success, nearly 50 members having enrolled and the local players evincing the most enthusiastic interest in the novel pursuit. The annual subscription is one guinea, but monthly tickets of membership are also issued.

The game is played with clubs and balls, the latter made of guttapercha and weighing about two ounces. The object of the game is, starting from the first hole, to drive the ball into the next hole in as few shots as possible and so on round the course, the player or players whose ball is holed in the fewest strokes being the winner of the game.

Each player is provided with an attendant, a 'caddie' who carries his clubs. He requires a set of clubs differing in shape to suit the position of the ball and the distance to be driven, crack players using as many as ten or twelve clubs. For the tryo, however, three or four clubs are a sufficient complement.

The onlooker who knows nothing of the game, is apt to consider it slow or even 'stupid' and has but to handle the club for half-an-hour to discover his mistake.

A recent writer says he never knew anyone commence to study this fascinating art and cease to follow it from having tired of it.

The knowledge of the game can only be acquired by much study and weariness of the flesh. An authority on the subject states that to play the game well requires long practice and very few attain to great excellence who have not played from their youth; but anyone, he says, may in a year or two learn to play tolerably so as to take great pleasure in the game.

There is this advantage, nevertheless, that both old and young may become golfers; and a more health-giving recreation is not to be found.

As the novice daily struggles over bunkers and sand-dunes, to say nothing of the 'desert' at Portrush, with the laudable ambition before him of reducing his odds from the duffer's liberal allowance to as near scratch as possible, he is breathing the purest atmosphere – the muscles both of the upper and lower limbs are equally exercised, the chest undergoes expansion and from the active exercise and inhalation of so much fresh ozone, the body is brought into the finest condition.

The charm and gain of all this, too, is the fact that the party engaged in play takes his pleasure and at the same time gains his vigour of body and mind unconsciously. It is a game which the vigorous youth may pursue quite as keenly as the septuagenarian – there are so many points to learn in which the smartest youth cannot attain proficiency without much practice."

To play the game well requires long practice and very few attain to great excellence.

"The additional portion of ground lately acquired by the Club was utilised for the first time and a course of fifteen holes was laid out for the competition, the first three being played a second time to complete the round. It was the general opinion that the new course was the most difficult that has yet been played over at Portrush and that the very utmost advantage had been taken of every feature of the ground. The competition winner was Mr Hugh Adair of Cookstown with a handicap of 15 and a net score of 87."

A press report from October 1890

CHAPTER 10

BOOST FOR THE 'BRIGHTON OF IRELAND'

*It will long be remembered as one of the most
successful Championships*

I T WAS A BOLD decision in 1951 and a turning point in the illustrious
history of The Open Championship. It placed the sporting spotlight firmly
on a small seaside town on the tip of the north coast of Ireland. For the first
time the most prestigious golf tournament in the world would be played at
a venue outside Great Britain. And the venue chosen by the Championship
Committee of the Royal and Ancient Golf Club of St Andrews – the beautiful
Dunluce links of Royal Portrush.

It was a massive boost not only for the Club but also for Portrush, the
'Brighton of Ireland' as it had been dubbed in the early part of the last century,
and still today, many people believe, the premier destination in Ireland for
those who like to combine a holiday by the sea with a round of golf.

If there was any element of gamble in the selection of Portrush for this
high honour, it did not materialise. Listen to the verdict of Frank Pennink,
one of the most respected golf correspondents of his day, in a piece he wrote
for *Golf Monthly*:

> "This year's Open Championship will long be remembered as one
> of the most successful ever held. It had so much to commend it; it
> ran smoothly, a British-born champion emerged; it was played on
> a truly magnificent links – perhaps the finest test of all our great
> courses – there were encouraging performances by young players and
> tremendous enthusiasm was shown by vast crowds. Indeed a happy
> first appearance in Ireland and Royal Portrush."

So on this score alone 1951 was a memorable year for Portrush and today
it still retains that accolade, that unique record in the staging of this great
Championship. Now that great Championship is making a welcome return

to the famous Dunluce championship course, acclaimed by many of the top professionals as one of the best, if not the best, in the world.

The history of Portrush as a golfing town is long and distinguished. At the turn of the last century, golf was one of its biggest attractions. Even then, according to an article in *Northern Ireland Illustrated*, one of a series of celebrated guide books published by W Mate & Sons Ltd, of Bournemouth (price one shilling), the links of the Royal Portrush Golf Club were regarded as "the St Andrews of Ireland."

"Persons of all ages and of both sexes," it was noted, "may enjoy the Royal and Ancient game under the pleasantest auspices, all requirements having been studied by the Club Council". It was observed also that "a long and short course over beautifully situated grounds afford fine accommodation, and the Ladies' and Gentlemen's Clubhouses want for nothing in equipment."

The charms of Portrush were: "...fully appreciated by not only the people of the North of Ireland cities, but by large numbers of English visitors, who come year by year to golf and bathe, to sail and fish, to tour on foot or on wheel, or as often as not to lounge in complete content along the cliffs and among the fragrant dunes, drinking in the sunshine and the pure air".

In the official guide book for Portrush, published by the Urban Council in the middle of the last century, it was proudly proclaimed that the Dunluce championship course had been described by many of the leading professional players as "one of the finest in the world."

Only Mother Nature, it was claimed, could have provided:

"...the close resilient turf, the unpurchaseable tonic of pure, bracing air, the impressive panorama of sea and coastline – characteristics which have made the Royal Portrush Golf Club the home of successive Irish Championships for many decades."

At the beginning of the last century, Portrush also occupied a unique position as a health resort. In June, 1904, a letter published in *London Opinion* declared:

"Jaded townsfolk would do well to consider the claims of this famous watering-place. It is but a little over twelve hours journey from London, including two hours by sea, via Stranraer and Larne. The air is marvellously invigorating and the breeze, sweeping in directly from the broad Atlantic, is peculiarly tonic in its effect. For attractions there is said to be, next to St Andrews, the finest golf course in the British Islands".

The main reason, however, was that the town had been "abundantly endowed by Nature with charms which influence all sorts and conditions of people."

Washed on three sides by the sea and sandwiched between two splendid beaches, the bracing and health-giving sea air was certainly a big factor and was promoted quite a lot in those days. In the words of an old poem:

Portrush is a pretty place, surrounded by the sea,
If it was cut from strand to strand, an island it would be.

In a fascinating book, *In Search of Ireland*, the distinguished travel writer, HV Morton, comments:

"It [Portrush] is built on a promontory that thrusts itself for three-quarters of a mile into the Atlantic and thus was designed by Nature as a perfect holiday resort."

His beautiful description of a sunset from an uninterrupted vantage point on Ramore Head is not only a fine piece of writing but also a definitive outline of the unique geographical location of Portrush:

"The sun was setting in the west. A few clouds were lying in the sky. They caught fire and burned for a little while in the bright red that faded to pink and grew dim and dun-coloured. I could see far to the west the faint blue hills of Donegal. When I looked north I could see the Western Isles of Scotland – Islay and Jura – and to the south of them the dim line of the Mull of Kintyre. It was a magnificent sight. The sea swept in over the sands in long, lazy half-moons; and as the light grew less, the sea was the colour of silver; the sands were grey and the afterglow throbbed and trembled in the sky. Mists hid Donegal, mists hid Scotland, and the first star lit the sky."

The situation of Portrush "practically next door to the Giant's Causeway which is generally classed as the eighth wonder of the world," was also very much in its favour.

A HOLIDAY HIGHLIGHT

Right up to its sad demise in 1949, a trip to this wonder of Nature from Portrush on the old Causeway tram would have been a highlight of a holiday in this part of the world. The official Portrush Guide carries an advertisement from the tramway company urging visitors that a tram ride was the best means of enjoying the magnificent scenery along the coastal route to the Giant's Causeway. There were frequent daily services connecting Portrush, Dunluce Castle and the Giant's Causeway with special rates for parties. The world's first hydro-electric tram was still a big draw.

The end was not too far off, I think, for the type of 'bucket and spade' holiday which had made Portrush such a popular place for a family trip to the seaside. It was still being played up in that old Guide book:

"…the sea is never more than a few yards away, it never completely covers the sand at full tide, and there is always ample room to make sand castles, stern fortresses and all the other things that an adept child with a bucket and spade can contrive".

Portrush was then a happy-go-lucky place where holidaymakers could meet up again year after year. Here's a little image of a sunny day on the beach:

"Paddling enthusiasts can have the time of their lives… and father can enjoy to the full the soporific effect of the daily paper, while mother discovers from another mother that domestic problems are the same in Glasgow as in Manchester, without having to worry about what the children are up to".

And finally, if any further evidence was needed to convince people that Portrush was the place for families to spend a brilliant seaside holiday, this:

"One of the finest sights you will see in this jolly town is the large number of sun-bronzed kiddies overflowing with robust health and good spirits".

I can vouch for the fact that, in those days, holidaymakers returned year after year and usually to the same hotel, guest house or boarding house. My mother took a great deal of pride in the fact that many of her guests returned again and again to spend their summer holidays in her establishment. I well remember the pleasure she got in the long winter months when the post arrived with letters from Belfast, Glasgow and many parts of England from old clients enclosing deposits to book their summer holidays well in advance.

I have been reading from a volume of Kahlil Gibran's *Collected Works* and one of the pieces struck a cord with me because it chimed very well with my memory of those old "golden strands" of Portrush:

I am forever walking upon these shores,
Betwixt the sand and the foam.
The high tide will erase my foot-prints,
And the wind will blow away the foam.
But the sea and the shore will remain
Forever.

A few months after all the drama and excitement of the 1951 Open Championship, a group of travel agents from the North of England paid a visit to Northern Ireland as guests of the Tourist Board and their last port of call was Portrush.

They were hugely impressed with the hospitality they had received throughout their visit and at a luncheon given in their honour by the Urban Council expressed "amazement" at the quality and variety of accommodation they had seen.

The pledge given was that they would endeavour to send as many people as they possibly could to Northern Ireland for a holiday visit.

They would surely have been impressed by one of the statistics given by the Town Clerk of Portrush, Mr WI Cunningham. He told them that in Portrush they had over 220 hotels and boarding-houses – more than were to be found in all the seaside resorts in Northern Ireland right round to Warrenpoint. That was a marvellous fact.

He concluded on a humorous note: "The resort is washed on three sides by the Atlantic. It has been said that the next townland to Portrush is America!"

CHAPTER 11
A SWEET SONG OF YESTERDAY

"In the good old summer time"

FRANK WAS HIS NAME, if I remember correctly, and for quite a few summers he was a familiar presence on the seafront at Portrush. A wily old photographer, he was adept at accosting visitors and persuading them, in the nicest possible way, to have their photograph taken. Frank –I never knew his surname – plied his trade back in the late 1940s and early 1950s when a trip to the seaside would not have been complete without being 'snapped' by Frank, or someone like him. It was still a novelty and part of the holiday experience.

His patter was irresistible so in the course of a day he must have taken scores of photographs. I'm sure there are hundreds of examples of his photographic skills still to be found in many an old family album. One of his favourite beats was the promenade overlooking the Arcadia and East Strand beaches. I don't remember precisely how it happened, but one beautiful, bright, sunny day I must have been a willing victim because I still have the photograph he took of me as a young boy striding purposefully along the sun-drenched promenade.

Perhaps he was having a slack day because I had encountered him many times and had always been able to pass without hindrance. Anyhow, I still have that old photograph and it remains something of a mystery. Where had I been? Where was I going? What had I been doing? I can't remember so I don't have the answers. There is a short inscription on the back but it doesn't help. All it says, in my reasonably good handwriting, is: "In the good old summer time" and the year it was taken, 1949. I would hazard a guess that it was a sort of veiled reference to the fact that since it was summer I did not have to worry about school. I was free to enjoy the pleasures and delights of carefree days in perhaps the most idyllic coastal region in Northern Ireland.

So a flood of nostalgia engulfed me when, for the first time in a good few years, I took a stroll along this promenade of dreams, re-living some of my boyhood days. In the distance, the Causeway headlands; on a clear day you can see parts of the Scottish coast and out in the bay, close to the shore, stand those guardian islands of Portrush, the Skerries. Apparently Skerries was the name, in the far distant past, by which Portrush was originally known.

The promenade has been given a massive face lift over its entire length from the small Arcadia beach to its end point along the East Strand, a distance of about a mile, as part of a regeneration plan for Portrush and I immediately gave it the thumbs-up.

The upgrade is striking and I feel that my home town now has a beautiful stretch of promenade that really sets off this part of the seafront. I am biased, of course, because this was my back yard when I was growing up. My mother's boarding-house was in Causeway Street, just a stone's throw away, so in the mornings I woke to the sound of the sea.

For me, getting onto the beach usually meant taking a running jump from the highest part of the promenade. It was great fun and I managed, nearly always, to land feet first on the soft, white sand. The new structure now boasts a fine sweep of gently graded steps so I wasn't tempted to try and replicate those old jumps!

I passed close to a derelict site where, when I was a boy, there had been a little shop selling ice-cream and sweets and coffee and a selection of seaside souvenirs. It was run by Mr and Mrs Forte and I remember them with fondness. They had another shop at the Causeway Street end of Main Street and the easiest way to get from one to the other was via the promenade. That is what I did quite a few times one summer when Mr Forte gave me a part-time job which involved carrying buckets of ice-cream in between the two shops.

The big shiny buckets had lids to prevent the liquid from spilling and I remember, with a friend, transporting them several times each day in hot weather when the sale of ice-cream was brisk. Just what the manufacturing process involved after the mix had been delivered remains a mystery to me to this day but one thing I can vouch for: the ice-cream which Mr Forte produced was delicious! It was sad to see the empty space where the little shop had been.

I'm not sure, but I think Mr Forte may also have had a franchise on deck-chairs because they were piled up just off the promenade, close to his shop, and on busy summer days they were hired out at a shilling a time, or was it sixpence? There was some money to be made by young boys and girls, myself included, in collecting deck-chairs which had been abandoned half-way along the beach by customers who couldn't be bothered to carry them back after a hard day lazing in the sun!

On my stroll along the promenade I stopped close to where, at the height of the summer, a little group of donkeys could be found most days. Mr Ramage was the gentleman who owned them and they were a familiar sight on this part of the East Strand. Youngsters like me were often recruited to lead the donkeys up and down the beach, usually at a slow, controlled pace, especially if very young children were on board. The donkeys were kept in a field at Ballywillan Road about half a mile away and this was something of a bonus for us boys – it was mostly boys who did the job – because after we had "saddled up", Mr Ramage allowed us to ride the donkeys down to the beach.

Donkeys have not been seen on the East Strand for many years but once they were very much part of the holiday scene and they are featured on many old postcards. Their names were written with pride on their bridles, names like Nellie, Molly, Billy and Jenny and children had their own particular favourites.

Years later I wrote a short story about an old beach donkey which had wandered off when its owner (the fictional counterpart of Mr Ramage) had fallen asleep during a quiet spell on the beach. 'Esmeralda's Kingdom' was broadcast as a Morning Story on BBC Radio 4 and for me the icing on the cake was that it was read by the very distinguished Ulster actor, JG Devlin. I've often wondered if he would have been aware of Esmeralda's Portrush pedigree!

Close to where the donkeys had huddled, and running along the base of the promenade, I came to the rock-pool where, armed with jam-pot and net, I used to search for crabs and John Doreys hidden in the swirling fringes of seaweed. It's the pool, also, where I learned to take my first tentative swimming strokes. In those days the water in the deepest part was just above my knees. Perhaps a plaque of some sort should be erected to mark the spot!

Bear with me. I've one more memory to share and, appropriately enough for a town like Portrush, it involves golf. A few months after Fred Daly had become the first Ulsterman to win The Open Golf Championship – he did it in 1947 – I achieved my own personal golfing goal.

My father had shortened an old, wooden-shafted driver so I could swing it more easily and for weeks I had been practising on the almost deserted winter beach. I would make a little tee of sand and the target I had set myself was to drive the ball from a spot just off the promenade so that it would reach the Tarry Burn, as it was known, a distance of between two and three hundred yards.

The water from this natural outlet made its winding way across the beach into the sea and one triumphant day my drive, a supreme effort, sent the ball rolling all the way up to the stream. I must confess that the distance the ball travelled probably had more to do with the hard, smooth surface of the sand than the power of my swing! Whether or not Fred Daly was the inspiration behind it, I'm giving him the credit anyway because, of course, he was born in Portrush and I was friendly with some of his nieces and nephews who were about my age and lived not all that far from me.

A huge sculpture, in the form of billowing sails, like those of a mythical fishing-boat – at least that's what I like to think – has been erected on a site overlooking the promenade and East Strand and it's a nice finishing touch. It reminded me of a beautiful line in one of Shelly's poems:

> My soul is an enchanted boat
> Which, like a sleeping swan, doth float
> Upon the silver waves of thy sweet singing.

As I left the promenade, and headed up towards Causeway Street, in my mind's eye I was still catching glimpses of old Frank, of Mr and Mrs Forte, of Mr Ramage and his donkeys, of Fred Daly, of a fresh-faced 14-year-old boy, and I thought to myself: yes, it really does feel as if my soul has been floating "upon the silver waves" of some very sweet singing indeed.

CHAPTER 12

HERE'S TO THE 'FLYING FOX' AND THE 'PORTRUSH LILY'

He was skilled both as a player and club-maker

IN THE EARLY 1950s, as a junior reporter learning the trade, I was given the responsibility of compiling the *Coleraine Chronicle's* 'Portrush Notes' column. This was one of my first assignments and it entailed calling each Thursday morning with prominent people in the community who had their finger on the pulse of the town, who knew what was happening mainly on the social scene from week to week. It was a task I quite enjoyed; it got me out of the office and gave me the opportunity of getting to know people who would later become valuable contacts in any breaking news scenario.

Meanwhile, I was content to gather as many community news items as possible, including whist-drive results and functions such as concerts and guest teas, sales of work, church services, all of which I tried to present in a factual and precise way, sometimes getting a nice angle on the story, good practice for a fledgling journalist.

One of the people I called with on a regular basis was a charming lady, Mrs LV Ross, who had a tobacconist and confectionary shop at the lower end of Main Street. Almost always she was able go supply some little morsel of news because of her involvement in community matters.

It was many years later that I learned that her father, Mr John Aitken, who died in 1916 at the early age of forty-three, had a distinguished reputation in Portrush and much farther afield as a golf club maker and who patented and manufactured golf balls as well. In fact, he was well known in golfing circles throughout the United Kingdom. He was the Royal Portrush Club's official club-maker and for a time was also the Club professional so he was skilled both as a player and club-maker.

A native of Edinburgh, John Veitch Aitken had come to Portrush in 1892 to act as club-maker to the Golf Club. It was a position he filled, his obituary records, "with marked acceptance and efficiency." It also notes that he was "an excellent player" as well.

Here is another quote from that source: "Being the oldest official of the Club, there was no one more familiar to visiting golfers and he will be greatly missed."

Mr Aitken belonged to a well-known golfing family in Edinburgh, two of his three brothers also being club-makers.

The *Derry and Antrim Year Book* for the year 1899 carries an advertisement from John Aitken, who also had his club and ball-making business at the Lower Main Street shop premises. It proclaimed the merits of his newly-patented golf ball, the 'Flying Fox' which had just made its debut.

No doubt the new ball was being tried out with gusto on the links of Royal Portrush under the watchful eye of Aitken. I like the name he gave to another golf ball invented by him – the 'Portrush Lily' – named after his daughter, Mrs LV Ross who all those years ago supplied me with little snippets of local news.

I have since learned also that this remarkable lady was a trained golf club maker herself, having acquired some of her father's skills, no doubt. In 1925 she had set up her own business in the Main Street shop which eventually became a very successful confectionary and tobacconist outlet.

Had I known then about her family's great golfing pedigree when I was calling into the shop many years later for those snippets of news for the Portrush Notes, I might have been tempted to ask her advice on how to improve my golf swing or how to play out of a bunker! Although I did play a little golf, I never took it all that seriously.

Mrs Ross died in February, 1987. Her obituary contained this fine tribute:

> "The passing of Mrs Ross brought to a close a life that made an immeasurable contribution to the town of Portrush and its people. She will be long remembered by those who knew her as a lady of great charm and sincere warmth, held in the highest regard by the entire community."

I understand that for a long time after her father's untimely death, caddies and golfers whose wayward tee shots ended up in the rough, were still finding some of those prized golf balls bearing the stamp 'Portrush' on one side and 'The Lily' on the other.

On the subject of golf balls, it was in the early part of the last century that a new type of ball, the 'Haskell', developed in America, came onto the market. It created quite a bit of excitement among golfers on this side of the Atlantic as well. Soon after its appearance it was used in a competition over the Royal Portrush links. This is how one golfing correspondent described it:

> "Differing from the solid form of the ordinary 'guttie', the Haskell ball is filled with rubber cord, and possesses in consequence greater resiliency or flying powers. But its present price is from 3s 6d to 7s 6d, and a cry has been raised in some quarters that the effect of its introduction will be to drive the poor man off the links, and that golf is rapidly becoming a rich man's game."

The new ball was certainly expensive when compared to the price of a remade 'guttie' which could be bought for just 7d. However, as was pointed out:

> "The present inflated price of the new ball is due to the demand being greatly in excess of the supply, but when the output has been increased, the market price will no doubt be fixed at a reasonable figure."

Golfers in Portrush, and indeed Portstewart, must have been among the first to try out the new ball because it was used for the first time in 1902 in a competition at Royal Liverpool by the great Sandy Herd who emerged victorious over the likes of Harry Vardon and James Braid. He was the only player in the field using the new ball.

Whatever impact the new Haskell ball had in Portrush, here's hoping that the 'Portrush Lily' and the 'Flying Fox' left their marks on this intriguing little piece of golfing history and that both were a flying success for John Aitken!

As a matter of interest, one of the balls made by him is on permanent display in one of cabinets in the Royal Portrush Clubhouse. It's nice to think that this tangible link with a unique piece of local golfing history has been preserved.

CHAPTER 13

A FORMIDABLE LADY OF THE LINKS

One of the area's best-loved sportswomen

IN THE SUMMER OF 1951, Portrush was getting ready to welcome some of the world's golfing greats. However, the town had its own home grown superstar in the person of Zara Bolton, who captained the 1956 British Ladies' Golf Team to victory against the Americans in the Curtis Cup for only the second time since 1932. It would be thirty years before they chalked up another win in this highly competitive event.

Mrs Bolton had a most distinguished pedigree in the Curtis Cup, having been first selected for the British team in 1948 and again in 1950 as reserve. She was non-playing Captain in 1956, 1966 and 1968 and Vice-Captain in 1958. Regarded as one of the area's best loved sportswomen, when she died at her home in Portrush in 1994 at the age of seventy-nine there was a great deal of sadness, particularly among the golfing fraternity.

She first came to Portrush as a member of the English Ladies' Golf Team. While here she met her future husband, Dr Sloan Bolton, who was hosting the welcome reception for the team, and later that year they were married.

Not surprisingly, perhaps, Mrs Bolton came from a golfing family. She started to play golf at the age of thirteen at Bishops Stortford in Hertfordshire.

She settled down to family life in Portrush – she had a family of four boys – and in 1948 she began to play competitive golf once more. In that year she won the Kent Championship and the Ulster Scratch Cup and was selected for the 1948 Curtis Cup team.

In September of that year she was narrowly beaten in the English Championship. Her last putt of the match rimmed the lip of the hole and failed to drop and victory went to her opponent, Miss Frances (Bunty) Stevens.

In 1951 she would doubtless have been thrilled with the announcement that The Open Championship was to be played at Royal Portrush. That year she received news that would have given her great personal satisfaction – she had been selected to go to South Africa as a member of the British Ladies' LGU Touring Team.

She won many international honours, having played in the home internationals seven times between 1939 and 1956 and was playing Captain in the 1955 event played at Royal Portrush, another accolade in her star-studded career which included a great record in the Ulster Scratch Cup. She won this cup on no fewer than six occasions.

At a local level, Mrs Bolton contributed much to the success and smooth-running of the Ladies' branch of Royal Portrush Golf Club. She had been President of the Ladies' Club from 1961 until the time of her death. She also served on the Irish Ladies' Golfing Union. She was chairperson of the Northern Executive and an Ireland representative on the Ladies' Golfing Union.

In spite of her commitment to golf at varying levels, Mrs Bolton found time for other interests and leisure pursuits. As her obituary writer noted:

"In addition to golf, Zara Bolton became, and remained, involved in many activities. She was an accomplished landscape painter in oils and made costumes for many years for the annual Portrush pantomime. She was a vice-president of the Royal British Legion, Portrush branch, and a dedicated committee member of Abbeyfield."

She was also described as "an enthusiastic participant" in every aspect of life, having the ability to listen and guide without criticism being "one of her most endearing qualities."

There is no doubt that her name will loom large for years to come in the annals of golf not only in Portrush but also in England where she grew up and where she learned to play the game so well.

The Ladies
Golf Club

CHAPTER 14

A MEMORY OF GOLDEN DAYS IN THE SUN

This will be one of the finest things ever to come to Portrush

WHEN IT WAS ANNOUNCED that Royal Portrush had been chosen as the venue for The Open Golf Championship in 1951 it was seen as a great sporting coup for the town as well as the Club. One of the most prestigious sporting events in the world was coming to town.

There was no sense of panic, either, because there was no need to spend thousands of pounds constructing new facades and covering up derelict and unsightly property in the resort. The reason for that, of course, was because – there weren't any.

The attitude was summed up by two of the leading citizens of Portrush at the time, the Urban Council chairman, Mr WR Knox, who confidently predicted: "Portrush will rise to the occasion," and by Captain WR Shutt, the man in charge of holiday entertainment in Portrush:

> "This will be one of the finest things ever to come to Portrush. The hotels may be full but there is still ample accommodation in our hundreds of guest-houses and boarding-houses."

Prior to the staging of the Irish Open Championship in 2012, some parts of Portrush had to be given a face-lift in order to project the best possible image for the thousands of visitors who would be attending such a prestigious event. That was seen as all the more important because of the tantalising prospect of attracting a re-staging of The Open on the Dunluce links.

It's interesting to recall that it was at Portrush that the Irish Open Amateur Championship was inaugurated in 1892, and the Irish Professional Championship in 1907. In 1895 it made another little piece of golfing history, being the first links outside England to stage the British Ladies' Championship.

In 1951, Portrush still retained much of the old world charm and atmosphere from its early Edwardian period. Its streets were lively and vibrant, its rows of boarding and guest-houses colourful and well-kept, its beaches pristine, and its bathing waters among the purest to be found anywhere. It was a magical summer place, still a Mecca for families from all parts. For a couple of weeks every summer there was a Scottish invasion, a link which had been well and truly established from the days when a passenger steamship service operated between the resort and Ardrossan.

For many years a good few of them ended up in my mother's boarding house in Causeway Street and my memory is that they were a jolly bunch. Many a Scottish air was heard being rattled out on the big upright piano in our living-room after supper on a sultry summer evening.

DANCING BY THE SEA

The Arcadia ballroom had not yet been built but there was dancing by the sea. Barry's amusements had a fine ballroom in those days and apart from a resident band some of the top bands from throughout the UK made special appearances from time to time.

Television had not yet come into our living rooms. It was still the age of the silver screen and in Portrush the Majestic Cinema and The Picture House, both on Main Street, were in full swing.

Barry's and Phil's Amusements catered for young and old, as is the case today indeed, and along with the various rides there were ample helpings of candy floss and popcorn and the mix that adds up to all the fun of the fair.

At that time diving displays at the Blue Pool, for so long a big part of the holiday programme in Portrush, were still a big attraction. Midnight diving displays, under powerful floodlights, were particularly spectacular and attracted huge numbers of spectators.

There was no denying the appeal of Portrush. Every day trains brought hundreds of visitors and trippers and when they disembarked at the railway station they found themselves right in the centre of the town. The Tudor style station was one of the jewels in the crown as far as Portrush was concerned. It was a very stylish building fronted by a spacious square and it was featured in many a picture postcard. Inside it had the beautiful smell and sounds of steam trains and the time was told by a splendid grandfather clock standing over twelve feet high, some say the tallest grandfather clock in the world. Thankfully it is still preserved and is now located just inside Barry's amusements arcade.

Jerry Locke pitching to the 7th Green.

Max Faulkner putting on the 10th Green.

Winner – MAX FAULKNER

1951
THE
OPEN
CHAMPIONSHIP

Perry Locke putting on the 18th Green.

Score-board at the Club House.

Memories of the 1951 Open at Royal Portrush.

Joyce Wethered, winner of the 1924 Ladies' Open Championship at Royal Portrush.

George C Nash, a famous Secretary of Royal Portrush.

Harry Vardon

Portrait in Royal Portrush of 'Old' Tom Morris of Open Championship fame.

Looking towards the first tee at Royal Portrush.

Peter Alliss in playing days.

Signed card sent from Peter Alliss to me along with his memories of the 1951 Open at Royal Portrush – "Keep swinging!"

Myself, caught on camera by Frank while striding purposefully along the sun-drenched promenade 'in the good old summer time'.

1951 – In the rough. I think I managed to chip out!

Bobby Locke approaching the ninth green in the 1951 Open Championship.

Fred Daly holds the Claret Jug after winning at the 1947 Open. The man on the right lifting him is none other than future winner Max Faulkner.

Portrush viewed from the golf course.

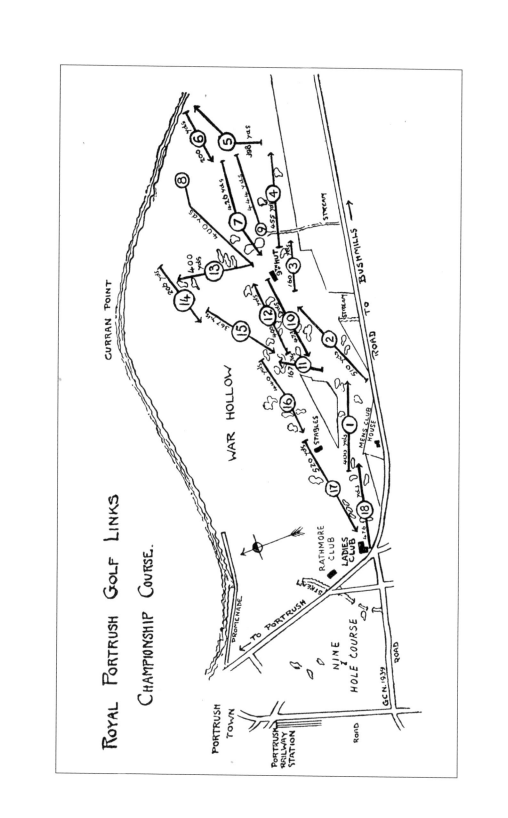

Checking the 1951 scoreboard beside the Clubhouse.

Bobby Locke in action.

Stylish Max Faulkner on his way to victory in the 1951 Open.

Max Faulkner with the Claret Jug.

Bobby Locke

Dai Rees

The three Portrush Miss Festival of Britain winners including, on the left, my sister Nan McAleese.

Old view of the West Strand.

The Children's Playground and the Arcadia in the 1950s.

A selection of
local adverts
from the period.

The Golf Hotel,

PORTRUSH.

FOR THE FAMOUS GIANT'S CAUSEWAY.

THIS HOTEL : : : is beautifully and conveniently situated.

It stands in its : : : Own Grounds which adjoins the Railway Station and extends to the Beach. : :

THE GROUNDS are BEAUTIFULLY LAID OUT.

EXTENSIVE : : VIEWS of SEA and LAND from all the Principal Rooms.

BOATING,

FISHING,

and DRIVING

can also be arranged for VISITORS.

TENNIS and CROQUET.

Overlooks the : :

LINKS OF THE ROYAL PORTRUSH GOLF CLUB.

Which are admittedly THE BEST IN IRELAND.

Terms Moderate : : and can be had on application to MANAGER.

Telegraphic Address—
" GOLFING, PORTRUSH."

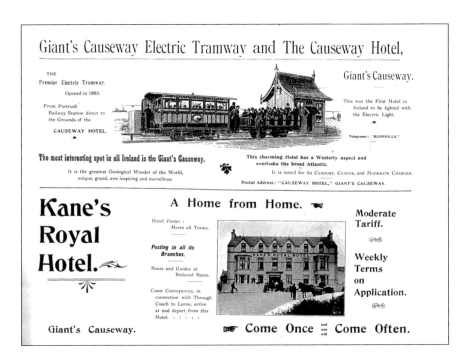

An official guide from the 1950s.

To Golfers.

Golfers will find all kinds of Clubs and Balls,
and every requisite of the game,
at the Depot of

John Aitken,

CLUB AND BALL MAKER TO THE

ROYAL PORTRUSH GOLF CLUB.

☞ Try his newly=patented Ball, "The Flying Fox."

BALLS RE=MADE, 2s 6d per Dozen.

REPAIRS NEATLY, CHEAPLY, & EXPEDITIOUSLY EXECUTED.

★ ★ ★ ★ ★ ★

TERMS MODERATE.

Walking Sticks, Tobaccos, Pipes, Cigars,
and Smoking Requisites in variety.

Main Street and Royal Golf Club, Portrush.

An advert from John
Aitken the famous
club and ball maker
at Royal Portrush.

Testing the Flying Fox

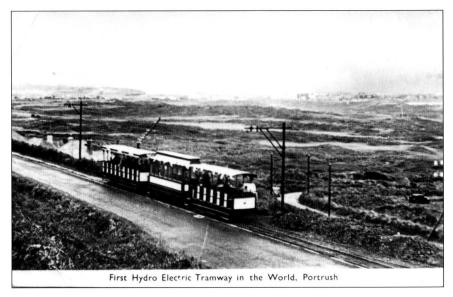

First Hydro Electric Tramway in the World, Portrush

Early photograph of the famous Causeway tram.

Portrush – a scene from the early part of the century.

The station building is still there but has now been converted into a factory shop and the square outside, once used as a go-kart track, has been thankfully redeemed and reinstated to something more like its former glory.

ARRIVAL OF THE DAILY BREAD

I have fond memories of the old station for another reason. In the summer of 1951 and for a few summers afterwards, I had to be at the station very early in the mornings. That was because I was a helper on one of McComb's bread-vans. The bread was delivered fresh from the bakery in Belfast each morning by train on large containers. From the containers it was loaded onto the bread-vans, not only McComb's but also the deliveries from the Inglis and Ormo bakeries as well. The bread-vans were environmentally friendly because they were battery powered and were charged overnight in the Portrush depot.

Back in 1951 there was one big fly in the ointment, at least as far as the town council was concerned and it had to do with the old Causeway tram. Another jewel in the crown of Portrush, it had come to the end of the line in 1949. The council had failed, in spite of strenuous efforts to keep it running, and was still smarting from that, so much so that it refused to have any kind of memorial erected, refusing the offer of one of the old carriages as a memento. To this day there is not a trace of this very significant piece of local history to be seen in Portrush.

Although much needed, the erection of an ultra modern bus station, not far from the railway station, was no consolation. In fact, it drew the wrath of some councillors because of its revolutionary design, its long flat concrete roof and open sides being likened to the deck of an aircraft-carrier.

So although the announcement about The Open golf was welcomed, councillors had other things on their mind. Portrush was in good shape; the golfing fraternity would be well catered for – there were no concerns whatever about accommodation. The town could boast quite a few first class hotels, including, of course, the Northern Counties. And almost every other house was a boarding or guest house. As yet caravans did not figure prominently on the holiday landscape.

My mother's boarding-house was in Causeway Street, little more than a stone's throw from the golf course and I remember that during the week of The Open she still had some vacancies. I think the same applied to a lot of the boarding-houses in Causeway Street and other parts of the town.

Now that the return of The Open Championship has been confirmed, there will inevitably be echoes of 1951, such a memorable year in Portrush, not only in its golfing history but also in its proud heritage as a place where, to quote an old poet, "waves sparkle like diamonds on ribbons of winding shoreline, leaving tide marks on the memory of golden days in the sun…"

Anyone who has ever spent a holiday in Portrush, especially in the early part of the 1950s, will surely have some golden memories of their own.

> "Portrush is a truly Open Championship golf course."
>
> *Sir Bob Charles, New Zealand professional golfer*

"COME BACK SOON TO PORTRUSH"

CHAPTER 15

A YEAR TO REMEMBER

End of the line for the old Causeway tram

FOR PORTRUSH, 1951 WAS a year to remember not only because of its big golfing coup but also because it marked the end of the line for a little piece of tramway history.

The Causeway tram ceased operating in 1949 and by 1951 the last section of the tramway track had been removed. Had it still been running, how nice it would have been for passengers to view some of the play in The Open Championship from its stately carriages as it trundled slowly along the fringes of the famous links on the road to and from Bushmills and the Causeway. The demand for tickets, I'm sure, would have been tremendous!

Passengers would certainly have had a unique grandstand view. They might possibly have been able to spot some of the most famous golfers of the day, like Bobby Locke, Henry Cotton and our own Fred Daly, winner of the Championship in 1947. The *Northern Constitution* of November 1949 recalled the opening of the line in 1883:

"That was a gala day in Portrush, Bushmills and throughout North Antrim and Derry. Vast numbers of people congregated at both ends of the system and along the entire coast road and were amazed to witness cars moving steadily and smoothly along without any visible means of propulsion – to them one of the wonders of the world. A waterfall at Walk Mills on the River Bush supplied power for the large dynamos which generated the electricity, conveyed to the tramway by wires, and has continued to do so to the present day with ample reserves."

Had it still been in operation in 1951 there would doubtless have been a few unofficial stops along the way to enable passengers to have a better sneak view of the action on the course! Or that the drivers might have reduced speed to a snail's pace at strategic points along the line.

I mention this because just a few years earlier, as a young boy, I remember travelling by tram to the Causeway with my father and, from one of the open carriages, waving to some of the golfers on the course. Perhaps my father knew some of them, although he did not play golf himself, or I may have known one or two of the caddies. It was a stunning picture postcard view over much of the course and the memory of that particular journey has stayed with me down through the years.

However, in spite of strenuous – some might even say heroic – efforts by Portrush Urban Council to save the old tram from the scrap-yard, the plug was pulled in 1949 and by 1951 the last remnants of the track were being taken up. It was indeed the end of an era. Here is another extract from the *Northern Constitution*:

> "The tramway was the favourite mode of coast travel for close on half-a-century; it was the delight of tourists; its amenities were enjoyed by all, rich and poor alike and many a romance which had its origins in a trip to the Causeway resulted in a happy married life."

Officially launched in 1883, the tramway was hailed as the first in the world to be powered by hydro-electricity. A trip to the Causeway by tram was the highlight of a holiday in Portrush for many years but towards the middle of the last century the number of passengers had begun to decline for a variety of reasons, including increased competition from other modes of transport.

So I suppose it could have been claimed, and probably was, that had the Causeway tram still been operational, The Open Championship, the biggest sporting event ever to be staged in Portrush, attracting thousands of visitors from all over the world, would have been a golden opportunity to show off its potential as a really major and important attraction in its own right. And, who knows, that might have been all that was needed to keep it going.

As it was, most of the tramway stock – carriages, engines and track – was sold off at an auction in Belfast in 1951, raising a total of just £11,000 which represented, I suppose, its scrap value at the time.

An interesting footnote is that Eastwoods, the scrap metal merchants contracted for the removal and disposal of the track and trams, offered

Portrush council one of the carriages, the idea being that it could be located somewhere in the town and preserved as a permanent memorial. But so upset was the council that its campaign to save the tramway had not produced the desired result, that the offer was declined. The *Northern Constitution* again:

> "Its closing will be regretted by thousands of people at home and abroad; by those who have prospered in other lands and by others whose lot is little better than it was when they left the golden shores and green hills of Antrim, but whose thoughts in nostalgic moments, will turn to the halcyon days of their youth and to the electric tramway making its way along the cliff road, through the sand-dunes to the Giant's Causeway."

Most visitors to Portrush did not leave without making the tram journey to the Causeway at least once. The track skirted some spectacular coastal scenery en route, notably the White Rocks and Dunluce Castle, and depending on the weather, one could opt for either an open-air carriage or an enclosed one.

Some of the tram drivers were well versed in local history and passengers might be given little snapshots from the past, particularly if the tram stopped at Dunluce, which it frequently did, to allow passengers a more prolonged view of the old castle ruins. Markets and fairs were formerly held at Dunluce and right up to the end of the eighteenth century they continued to be held in November each year. They were then transferred to the town of Bushmills because they had become "a depot for rioting, gambling, drinking and sundry other vices".

The attraction of the old Causeway tram is strikingly illustrated in one small statistic dating back to a July day in 1913 when no fewer than 3,200 passengers "passed over the line", creating a record for the tramway. From the *Northern Constitution*:

> "Perhaps Mr Traill [its founder] was in advance of the times but his researches and discoveries will be assessed at their true value when electricity becomes one of the dominant forces of the world. In a lesser degree, the present generation will remember with gratitude that he opened the way for hundreds of thousands of tourists who annually visit our shores to explore and enjoy the beauties of North Antrim and its magnificent coastline, as well as for the resident population to whom these glories were hitherto unknown."

That summer of 1913 it was reported that traffic on the electric tramway had been exceptionally good. "All the available cars," it was announced, "have been steadily on the move, conveying crowds of holidaymakers to and from the Giant's Causeway."

Sometimes the journey could be quite hazardous, as this extract from an old news report clearly indicates:

> "Conductors at this season of the year have many exciting experiences owing to negligence of persons passing over the tramway line. On Wednesday last a man belonging to Coleraine, who was in charge of a horse and van, had a narrow escape when emerging from the laneway emerging from Dunluce Castle. The bell was sounded but the horse was just about to be driven over the line in front of the tram when Mr Samuel Campbell, who was in charge, instantly applied the brakes and stopped the car, thereby averting a serious collision".

Also reported that summer was an incident in which a small pony and trap collided with the tram opposite the railway station in Portrush. Again it was a case of a narrow escape because the pony was only slightly injured in its forelegs while the occupants of the trap were unhurt.

The skilful driving of Mr Samuel Campbell was again highlighted in another incident near Dunluce. He was at the controls on his way to the Causeway when the hand-brake slipped and, swinging round, struck him sharply on the forearm. Although suffering great pain, he remained at the controls. One report of the incident stated:

> "…he would not give in and actually brought the tram to the Causeway and back to Bushmills before he could be persuaded by his colleagues to leave what he considered his post of duty".

Later he was examined by a doctor and it was found that his arm was badly broken below the elbow.

Those were relatively minor incidents compared to the tragedy which occurred in the summer of 1903 involving the deaths of two children. This extract from the company's annual meeting explains what happened:

> "Two children lay down on the bank of the line at a curve where they could easily have been seen if standing, and fell asleep, and waking up suddenly after the engine had passed them, were killed by the car following."

The company was not held to blame for the accident at the coroner's inquest which followed. However, an action for damages was taken by the parents of the children and although having no legal responsibility, the company, it was reported, "thought it best to settle the case for £75..."

To this day, not a trace is to be found in Portrush of that unique and historic old tramway which for so many years was linked with the history of the place. What a pity.

CHAPTER 16

THERE WAS A GREAT BUZZ ABOUT THE CLUBHOUSE

I remember seeing some of the world's top players in action

Acommercial traveller from Belfast who regularly stayed at my mother's boarding house in Causeway Street, was a keen golfer and one evening after tea he said to me, "Maurice, let's take a run down to the Golf Club and see what's happening with the golf."

I don't remember whether it was one of the practice days or if the Championship was actually under way but anyway we drove down to the Golf Club in his little Morris Minor and again, if my memory serves me right, we were able to drive straight into the Clubhouse carpark with no bother at all.

Not too many people owned cars then and the traffic was nothing like today. We were able to watch some of the players, some on the practice ground and others on the putting green. There was a great buzz about the Clubhouse but everything was relaxed and there didn't seem to be much security in evidence.

I was very familiar with the Championship course and the Valley course because I had caddied for a little while and even played for a time on the smaller Valley course. I don't know how much tickets for spectators were in those days but that wasn't something that worried me unduly because I knew all the best places to sneak onto the course and it was easy to lose myself in the crowds and keep out of the way of the stewards. I offer a belated apology for that now but I still enjoy telling the story!

In a funny sort of way, my little subterfuge added to the thrill and excitement of the occasion and I remember seeing some of the top players of the day in action. Players like the great Henry Cotton, Bobby Locke, Florrie van Donk, Fred Daly and of course the winner, Max Faulkner, who cut a flamboyant dash because of the bright colours he wore.

A SHOT TO REMEMBER

For me, the shot of the Championship was played by an American competitor, Frank Stranahan, and I was lucky because I was quite near the green so I had a grandstand view. It was at the 17th hole which is close to the ladies' Clubhouse. He played a beautiful approach shot and his ball landed in the middle of the green but rolled about 20 feet past the hole.

However, there was so much backspin on the ball that it pulled back, as if on a string, to within a couple of feet of the hole. I've never forgotten that shot. I think Stranahan was one of the few amateur players in the Championship and he acquitted himself well, completing all four rounds and finishing near the top of the leader board. In fact, he won the Silver Medal for the highest finishing amateur. He later turned professional.

I do remember that on one of the Championship days I had to leave the course early because a friend of mine and a friend particularly of my sister Nan, was emigrating that day to Australia. She was travelling with a local family who were also Australia bound under the £10 assisted passage scheme.

It was a regular occurrence in those days and the point of departure was the railway station. Usually a big crowd of friends and well-wishers gathered to wish them bon voyage. For me it's still a poignant memory, all the more so, I suppose, because of the link it has with the Golf Championship. It gives another small insight into how life was in those days, how different things were. In 1951 Portrush was still a special place, a place where a little bit of golfing history was made.

DOWN TO THE GOLF

In 2012 I was lucky enough to be present every day during the Irish Open Championship, staged so successfully at Royal Portrush. This time I was a paying spectator! I was caught up in the hustle and bustle and the whole mesmerising atmosphere but every so often, during lulls in between play, I found myself slipping back to 1951, remembering what it was like then. There were flashing images of those old forgotten fairways, of Max Faulkner and Fred Daly, of Bobby Locke and Henry Cotton and some of the more peripheral mists of time began to lift also for some strange reason.

For instance, I suddenly remembered the name of the commercial traveller who had brought me "down to the golf" that evening – Mr Williamson – and it came back to me also that the commodity he travelled the country seeking orders for was Kraft cheese. Needless to say there was always a plentiful supply of it in our house because Mr Williamson was generous with his discount.

After my little reverie on the golf course, Mr Williamson figured again in a dream I had that same night. I had just won the British Open and he was presenting me with the Claret Jug. I was acknowledging the cheering crowds when I realised that the trophy I was holding aloft had a strange feel to it. When I examined it more closely I discovered it was made of – cheese. Then I woke up!

Forgive me for that little diversion but what can I say? It's still a pleasant memory after all these years, one of my own 'fairways of delight' you might say. I'm not sure if they still make Kraft cheese today. I would never have admitted it to Mr Williamson, of course, but I didn't really like it all that much.

Bobby Locke, the world famous South African golfer, failed in his bid in the 1951 Open to make history by winning the Championship for the third year in a row. He was, the *Irish News* reported, "a slightly sad man when he finished equal sixth with an aggregate of 293 (71, 74, 74, 74). But sportsman that he is, he was one of the first to offer his hand in congratulations to the new champion."

View from the
17th fairway

CHAPTER 17

LETTERS TO THE SECRETARY OF A GOLF CLUB

The Portrush connection

B Y 1951, BARELY INTO my teens, I was very familiar with a classic and extremely humorous book with a strong Portrush connection, *Letters to the Secretary of a Golf Club* by George C Nash. I had discovered it by accident one day in the well-stocked bookcase which my mother kept in the drawing-room, mainly for the convenience of our boarding-house guests. The bookcase contained a wide selection of books and I suppose she felt that, as we were so close to the golf course, it would be good to have one or two books about golf on the shelves. I think she was right because my memory is that the Nash book was one of the most widely read.

There is another reason, although I cannot be sure of this, and it is that my mother and father may well have known the author because back in the 1930s he was Secretary of the Royal Portrush Golf Club and would, presumably, have been quite a well-known personality in the town.

I'm not suggesting that any of the characters who inhabit the pages of his *Letters* books (I think he wrote three in all) were based on real people, but his job must surely have provided him with some invaluable snatches of insight and inspiration.

All the letters are addressed to the long-suffering secretary of Roughover Golf Club, Patrick Whelk, and the pages are filled with letters from the likes of Lionel Nutmeg, formerly of the Malaysian Civil Service; James Duffit, Ezekiel Higgs, Colonel Fortescue and R Bindweed, to name but a few. Being a fine artist, Mr Nash also provided some of the illustrations for the books. In 2011 a small watercolour he did in 1942 of the famous sixth green, with the White Rocks and Causeway headlands in the background, was auctioned at Bonham's in London, and sold for £480.

For many years he contributed a regular column in *Punch* magazine and in fact much of the material in the books first appeared in the magazine. It is said – and it's fairly obvious from his writing – that he had "fine powers of observation and incisive wit."

GOLF IN NORTHERN IRELAND

It was not too surprising, then, when he was asked by the Northern Ireland Tourist Board to write an introduction for a very attractive little guide book entitled *Golf in Northern Ireland,* published some time in the 1950s, I think. No better man to extol the virtues of the game and he did so with finesse, nailing his colours to the mast from the outset: "…few countries in the world can offer the holidaymaker such an astonishing variety of sport in so compact a space."

Royal Portrush, he declared, stood "bold and magnificent beside the famous Giant's Causeway" while Newcastle's Royal County Down nestled "in the shadow of the lovely Mountains of Mourne."

At the time there were some sixty golf courses in Ulster, comprising "every sort and shape of lay-out that might well be conceived." Most of the courses had been constructed on modern lines, and the architectural genius of such well-known men as Colt and Braid "are manifest in several places." In fact, Colt one of the top golf course designers, had been called upon in 1933 to redesign the Dunluce links. He said afterwards that it was one of the best lay-outs he had ever designed.

Mr Nash was also at pains to point out how easy it was to get to Northern Ireland from the mainland. Few people, he declared, who had not travelled there, appreciated how soon the journey could be accomplished either by air or sea routes. One example he gave: a golfer could leave London at 6 or 7 pm, or even later, and be on the first tee of the majority of Ulster courses in time for a round before lunch the next day.

Fully ninety per cent of the golf courses in Northern Ireland were laid out in very beautiful surroundings. Where, he asked, would you find the equal of Castlerock and Portstewart, by the blue-gold shoreline of the Atlantic; of Ballycastle, set in one of Ulster's loveliest bits of country; of Cushendall, half surrounded by the Glens and lovely mountains of County Antrim; and of Larne, perched on a hill, with views of the Isle of Man and Scotland?

I think the Tourist Board got good value for their money from Mr Nash! Immediately below his by-line the information was given that he was 'GCN' of *Punch* and author of several books on golf.

ANOTHER LINK WITH PORTRUSH

Letters to the Secretary of a Golf Club was published in 1935 when Nash would, in all probability, still have been in his Royal Portrush job. It was certainly his most famous book. Interestingly, some 65 years later, Rhod McEwan Publishing brought out a reprint and it was launched, very successfully, at the Muirfield Open in 2002.

The book has yet another fascinating link with Portrush. The same publishing firm produced a facsimile to the book's original specification in a limited edition of just 51 copies. It is known as the Portrush edition and what makes it even more special is that it now also contains a foreword by the present Secretary of Royal Portrush Golf Club, Wilma Erskine. Each copy has been signed by Ms Erskine and I'm sure it is highly prized by anyone lucky enough to own one. Incidentally, it also contains a reproduction of a very fine pencil sketch of the author which hangs in the Royal Portrush Clubhouse.

A COLOURFUL AND FLAMBOYANT SECRETARY

Although not in the same class as George Nash, one of the most colourful and flamboyant secretaries of the Royal Portrush Club in former times was a gentleman called Charles Vint. He was the man in charge in the early part of the last century and he seems to have had a highly individualistic approach to his job.

A Dublin visitor had been so impressed by Mr Vint that when he returned home he wrote a letter to a magazine called *Motor News* singing his praises. Perhaps this gentleman, or lady, had been on a motoring holiday. Using the initials 'JCP' this is what he, or she, wrote:

> "Then there is the golf, which is of excellent quality. If I were asked I would place the Portrush links in the first three Irish courses. There is a ladies' links inside the big course – a links within a links – and it is always well patronised.
>
> "Speaking of golf reminds me that the Portrush club is very fortunate in having an ideal Secretary in Mr Charles Vint. You may go there a stranger but thanks to Mr Vint's courtesy and tact, you are not there many hours until you feel yourself incorporated into the happy family. If caddies are short, Vint comes to your rescue. Should you require a partner, he does the needful.

"In all my experience I never met a better official, and in expressing this view I am only voicing the opinions of scores of visitors I met during my stay.

"Not only does he look after all your requirements but he is a terror for entertaining. His one big mission in life seems to be making his guests happy and in our case he more than succeeded. Herein lies the great secret of success in connection with this old-established club."

BEST HOSTELRY IN IRELAND

The same person must have been staying in the Northern Counties Hotel while in Portrush because there were some highly complimentary remarks about the manager, Mr Frank Audinwood. The hotel had an arrangement with the Golf Club that its guests could have free use of the fairways, a considerable fillip in those days. Anyway, 'JCP' wrote:

"Then there is the Northern Counties Hotel, which is unquestionably the best hostelry in Ireland. Not only is it sweet and clean, but the food is of excellent quality and the officials are all courteous. In this respect they take their cue from the manager, Mr Audinwood, who displays a fatherly interest in every guest.

"In the Northern Counties everything goes like clockwork. There is no fuss or excitement, for behind the scenes there is a first-class organising brain. Little wonder that some of the guests we met there had not missed a season for ten or twelve years. Folks like going where things are good and where they are well served."

The concluding paragraph of the letter gives a nice little insight into the wider aspects and attractions of a holiday in Portrush at that time:

"For instance, the cliff scenery is particularly fine, especially on the run to the Giant's Causeway and Ballycastle. On the Derry side, too, there are some exquisite bits of wild, rugged coastline that would be hard to match.

"Then the roads – and this will interest motorists – are far above the average. Even when very narrow the surface is invariably good. Above and beyond everything else, the air is like a tonic – you feel it doing you good whether motoring, golfing, walking or swimming. Portrush has a great asset in its ocean air."

If Portrush had wanted to pay someone to compose a holiday brochure about its delights and attractions, then 'JCB' would have been a good candidate for the job. In another part of the letter, for instance, the writer compares the air to "a kind of atmospheric champagne!"

The observations about bathing are equally interesting and informative and again a fascinating picture is painted:

> "The bathing, both in the Blue Pool and the Harbour, is of the finest quality. The water is so buoyant and so stimulating that it makes you feel glad to be alive. The Blue Pool is one of the sights of the place. There you see some pretty diving from high rocks, to say nothing of spring boards and water chutes.
>
> "They are advanced enough in Portrush to have mixed bathing, which seems to give the ladies much confidence. I hear the project was only carried at the local council by one vote. Now, however, that the system is established, he would be a bold man who would attempt to revert to the old order.
>
> "In the Blue Pool they bathe in singles, in pairs and in family parties, with hundreds of spectators sitting round the natural amphitheatre. The watchers seem to enjoy the proceedings almost as much as the bathers."

Some personal reflections are given on the subject of mixed bathing, something which was still very controversial at the time.

> "What harm prudish people find in mixed bathing I could never comprehend, unless it can be put down to that old, deep-rooted objection some people entertain to seeing others enjoying themselves. I am acquainted with most of the bathing resorts around the Irish coast, but I know of none where the bathing facilities are as good as the famous Blue Pool."

As with most resorts, the pattern of bathing has changed over the years and the Blue Pool has not been used for bathing for a very long time. But in the middle of the last century it was still a big attraction in Portrush, having a 'blue lagoon' appeal about it. And it's not beyond the bounds of possibility, surely, that some of the competitors in The Open would have taken the plunge into its inviting depths. It would have been good for relaxing muscles and improving swings!

CHAPTER 18

IN THE FOOTSTEPS OF GIANTS

There was quite a bit of controversy about the shoes

I WAS SOMEWHERE IN the crowd gathered around the last green at Royal Portrush Golf Club when Max Faulkner rolled in his last putt to win that historic 1951 Open Championship. A teenager then, I had no sense that history was being made in Portrush that day – it was Friday 6 July – but indeed it was and the reason, of course, was that for the first time in its illustrious history, this ancient and venerable Championship had been played at a venue outside the British mainland.

I don't remember if Max Faulkner, in his great moment of triumph, threw the ball into the crowd as often happens on such sporting occasions, providing a coveted souvenir for some lucky spectator. I do know, however, that the ball he was playing with was a Dunlop 65 with the number 2 stamped on it. The reason I know this is that it now forms part of a prized collection of golf and other memorabilia in the possession of local man and keen golfer, Niall O'Boyle.

It is not the only 'trophy' he has from that great 1951 Championship. A member of Portstewart Golf Club, where the qualifying rounds were played, Niall is also the proud owner of the very shoes worn by Max Faulkner when he strode majestically over the Dunluce links and into golf's history books, notching up his one and only Major title in a long and distinguished career.

Later he would describe his win at Portrush as his greatest achievement. He said: "It was all I ever wanted. The Open meant everything to me." Going into the last round he led the field by six shots and so confident was he of winning that he was reported to have added, after his autograph, "1951 Open Champion".

Perhaps he had some kind of premonition because he later claimed that during his round he had been helped by "a mysterious light". Be that as it may, he went on to finish with a score of three under par, two strokes ahead of his nearest rival, Antonio Cerda.

So Max Faulkner's next visit to Portrush, in 1995, was surely an emotional one, the more so because it coincided with his 79th birthday. He was accompanied by his wife, Hilary, along with some friends and other relations. The icing on the cake came when his son-in-law, Brian Barnes, competing in the Senior Championship for the first time, lifted the trophy. It was a case of celebrations all round.

When I met up with Niall O'Boyle at his home in Portstewart, he told me the fascinating story of those Open golf shoes, just part of his unique collection which also includes a multi-autographed copy of the official programme for the first two days of the Championship, now extremely rare and highly prized by collectors. And yes, among the autographs is one by the man himself, Max Faulkner.

In pristine condition, the steel spiked golf shoes, with leather soles and leather uppers, finished in navy and white, look as if Max Faulkner might have just stepped out of them. One of the shoes bears his autograph, making them even more of a novelty.

AN INTRIGUING TALE

It all began with Niall's father Jim, who for almost forty years was proprietor of the Crown and Shamrock Inn or O'Boyle's Bar as it was better known, in Kingsgate Street, Coleraine. Niall explained:

> "My father was not only a publican but also an avid collector of antiques and all sorts of bric-a-brac and much of what he accumulated went on display in the bar. It was always a talking point among customers and over the years some of them even donated bits and pieces and so it built up into quite a collection."

One day in 1951 the conversation was all about The Open golf in Portrush and a man in the bar got everybody's attention when he said he would be caddying at the event. As he was leaving, the genial host jokingly quipped: "Don't forget to bring us back a souvenir from the golf!"

It turned out that the player he was caddying for was none other than Max Faulkner. Following his triumphant win, Faulkner made a gift of his golf shoes to his caddie as a memento of the occasion. And the rest, as they say, is history… almost. That was not the end of the story. Some time afterwards the Royal Portrush Club staked a claim to the shoes and it was a while before the dispute was sorted out. In the interim the shoes were kept in custody in the local police station!

"There was quite a bit of controversy about the whole thing at the time," recalled Niall, "but it all ended well and the caddie was able to keep the shoes."

A letter written and signed by The Open Champion himself confirmed the generous gift. And some time later the famous shoes were acquired by Niall's father and put on permanent display in Coleraine's Crown and Shamrock Inn. A step in the right direction, you might say! I'm sure the amusing story of how they came to be locked up in a police station was told many times down through the years.

MAX REUNITED WITH HIS SHOES!

There is yet another twist to this intriguing tale, surely one of the most poignant and moving in the history of golf. It takes us back to the summer of 1995 when the Senior British Open Championship was being played over the Dunluce links. After a lapse of some 44 years, Max Faulkner was back in Portrush, not as a player this time, but as a spectator and surely it must have been a time of great nostalgia for the former champion. He was made an honorary member of the Royal Portrush Club on that occasion and, courtesy of Niall O'Boyle, was re-united with his 1951 golf shoes!

The story had been picked up by a Radio Ulster sports team and they were on hand to record the moment. Both Max and Niall were interviewed by sports reporter/producer Rod Nawn, a former colleague of mine. "It was such a pleasure to meet Max Faulkner," said Niall. "I thought he was a perfect gentleman and he was delighted to autograph the shoes for me. He was highly amused by the whole story."

Niall's father was not a golfer himself so that's a little touch of irony. When he retired in 1978 it also marked the end of the pub which had been such a landmark in Coleraine for so many years and the nearest thing to a mini museum in the town. When the doors were closed for the last time, the curtain was brought down also on a novel and highly unusual showcase, reflecting in a unique way, so many aspects of sporting and social history.

Now, in what can be seen as a beautiful tribute to his father's memory, Niall has converted part of the roof-space of his home into an almost exact replica of the old family pub/museum with some of the original fixtures and fittings and, of course, many of the exhibits back on display, including those famous golfing shoes. Meanwhile, he has added a few more items to the collection, such as a framed and autographed photograph of Portrush golfer Graeme McDowell proudly holding the US Open Golf Championship trophy which he won in 2010 as well as a signed pennant from the Pebble Beach Golf Club where the Championship was held.

Needless to say, the little bar which Niall has created, atmospheric and evoking a host happy memories, is the ideal spot for family gatherings and special occasions, a place where the old days can be recalled and, for anyone interested in golf, old fairways brought back to life again. I'm sure Max Faulkner, who died in 2005 at the age of 88, would have approved.

"…he was delighted to autograph the shoes for me."

Niall O'Boyle

Max Faulkner's 1951 Open Championship medal was listed for sale at an auction in Sotheby's in July 1995 the year, incidentally, when Faulkner returned to Portrush for the Senior British Open Championship, not as a player but as a spectator – his son-in-law, Brian Barnes won the Championship that year. However, the medal, which had a price tag of between 30,000 and 45,000 euros, was subsequently withdrawn from the sale.

CHAPTER 19

SWEET DREAMS IN CAUSEWAY STREET

It was a good time to be growing up in Portrush

O N THE COAST ROAD, mid-way between Portrush and Bushmills, there is a cliff-top car park from which stunning views may be had of the White Rocks and the famous Dunluce golf links, set against the hazy spires and misty rooftops of Portrush and in the far distance, the faint, blue outline of the Innishowen headland.

I was fortunate. On the day I parked there not so long ago, the 'gentleness of Heaven' was on the sea, waves were breaking noiselessly on the broad sweep of the East Strand and a tiny yacht just off the Skerries was barely moving in the shimmering and glistening grandeur.

Lost in the beauty of the scene, I imagined I could pick out the rooftop of the house in Causeway Street where I had lived with my parents and my older sister and two younger brothers.

ERA OF HOPE AND PROSPERITY

It was a good time to be growing up in Portrush. I'm talking about the decade or so leading up to that big Open golf event in 1951. By then the town had just about shaken off its wartime austerity. There was a mood of optimism. A new era of hope and prosperity was beckoning and although I was too young to be aware of it at the time, you could say that in Portrush it was kicked off with the staging of that historic Open golf championship.

We lived not all that far from the golf course. More importantly as far as us youngsters were concerned, our house was just a few doors away from the Seaside Supply Stores, a grand-sounding name for what was, in effect, a small confectionary and tobacconist shop. It also stocked a selection of groceries and, in the summer time, an array of buckets and spades and other essential paraphernalia for the beach.

The interior was like an Aladdin's Cave. I was mesmerised by the number of big glass jars lining the wall behind the counter, full of mouth-watering sweets of all shapes and colours, including clove rock, brandy balls, liquorice all-sorts and dolly mixtures. We bought them usually in quarter pounds and Mr Stockman, the genial and jovial proprietor of the Seaside Supply Stores, was adept at weighing the sweets on a big set of scales and flicking open, with one hand, a paper bag to put them in. Saturday night was always 'sweets night' in our house, a special treat we enjoyed, particularly on dark winter evenings while playing a game of Snakes and Ladders or Monopoly.

The Seaside Supply Stores was not the only outlet for sweets on our street. Mr Brody had a similar, but somewhat smaller, outlet farther along and he stocked some brands not available elsewhere so naturally he got some of our custom as well. And apart from that, Mr Brody, if he was in a good mood, would occasionally throw in an extra sweet or two for good measure!

Close by was the All-Cash Stores, a grocery shop where sides of bacon were sliced before your very eyes on a lethal looking machine mounted on top of the back counter. This operation was usually carried out by Mr Moore, a gentleman of the old school who had a hearty laugh and enjoyed a bit of chat with the customers. My mother was a regular customer of his and during the summer her weekly grocery order would be delivered by a boy on a message-bike with a huge wicker basket mounted on a frame just above the front wheel.

NEW USE FOR A PAPER CONE

People living along this part of Causeway Street were certainly spoiled for choice as far as shops were concerned because there was yet another within a stone's throw from where we lived – yes, it was also a confectionary shop. It was located just across the road from St Patrick's Primary School, which I attended, so it was a sort of unofficial tuck shop for the pupils. I don't remember if it had a name but it was owned by an elderly gentleman, Mr Mackle.

I was always fascinated to see how expertly he could take a square piece of brown paper and fashion it into the shape of a cone into which he poured the sweets after having meticulously weighed them, retrieving the one or two that had tipped the scales over the mark. It was not long after the war and

I suppose the use of a paper cone was one way of coping with some of the wartime restrictions, including rationing, still in place at the time.

With so many sweetie shops in Causeway Street when I was growing up I suppose a little bit of over indulgence now and again could be excused; however, my mother kept a fairly close eye on us and made sure that it did not happen on a regular basis.

All of these shops were within a few hundred yards of our house. There was also a motor garage, McCaughan's, practically next door although, like most people in the street, we did not have a car. Plenty of people had bicycles and sure enough, Causeway Street had a bicycle repair shop just around the corner from where we lived. It was in the Old Forge, a cul-de-sac entry off Causeway Street where there were also a few houses. Mr Molloy could repair and build bicycles and his workshop was packed to the brim with bicycle parts and bicycles in various states of repair. He got plenty of business and was always hard at work any time I called, mostly to get him to fix a puncture. He would allow me to stay and watch him at work and I loved the atmosphere and the oily aroma of the place and the large selection of tools he had at his command.

An interesting footnote: I discovered recently that Fred Daly's father, who was a blacksmith, worked at Simpson's Forge which was an offshoot of Causeway Street, so I guess that link was preserved in the name Old Forge.

Another craftsman close at hand was Mr Nimmock, a highly skilled cobbler, who had a little boot and shoe repair shop practically next door to McCaughan's Garage. Many a time I was sent to him with a pair of shoes or boots badly in need of new soles and heels and when they had received his magic touch they were almost like new. I remember him as a man who seemed very happy and content in his work, who spent his working day surrounded by piles of boots and shoes awaiting his attention. He went about his work meticulously and obviously got a great deal of satisfaction out of it.

Although it was only a short distance from our house, I often cycled to the Post Office to post a letter or, more infrequently, to lodge some money in my savings account. Portrush had a palatial Post Office then. Apparently one of the reasons for this was that in the early part of the last century the White House department store on Main Street operated a huge mail order business, daily despatching items of Irish linen and tweeds and a wide selection of other goods to all parts of the globe.

DANCING THE NIGHT AWAY

Close to our house, too, stood the Palladium Ballroom, a popular dance venue in the summer months. Victor Sylvester, Ted Heath and Joe Loss were some of the big names appearing there with their dance bands from time to time. It was a ballroom of romance on our doorstep – sometimes at night when we were supposed to be asleep, we could hear the music, mainly waltzes, quick steps and fox trots and if it was Joe Loss, some jazz. In winter the ballroom was used for community events as well, including whist drives, concerts and badminton.

In the years just after the war, horse-drawn traffic could still be seen on the streets of Portrush, although this had begun to tail off (pardon the pun) by 1951. Coal, bread, milk and general groceries were all delivered by horse and cart. I remember a farmer, Mr White, from a short distance outside the town, who had a horse-drawn buttermilk cart, calling with my mother each week. His customers would bring their own containers, jugs, buckets or any other suitable vessel to hand which he filled from a small tap at the rear of the cart. The buttermilk was always cool and fresh and my mother was particularly fond of drinking a glass just after it had been delivered, maintaining that it had excellent medicinal qualities and we were always encouraged to try some. A friend of our family, a retired surgeon who had spent most of his working life in England, agreed and he also enjoyed a glass of buttermilk if he happened to call at or about the time of a fresh delivery.

THE TIDE YIELDED UP UNEXPECTED TREASURE

Where we lived in Causeway Street was just a hop, skip and a jump from the East Strand and whether it was winter or summer, it had all sorts of pleasures and delights to offer. In summer we changed into our swimming trunks at home and ran down to the beach, plunging into the waves within a minute or two. And then, to dry off, a vigorous run along the shoreline. It was a fantastic playground to have so close at hand and we took full advantage of it.

After a winter storm the tide would have washed up an array of flotsam and jetsam which had to be investigated and sometimes it yielded up unexpected trophies. I remember on one occasion finding lumps of coal strewn along a section of the beach, probably discarded for some reason or other from a passing coal boat. I filled a few buckets and it kept the home fires burning for a good while.

Portrush still had its own gasworks in those days and you're right – they were located at the bottom of Causeway Street where it joined with Bushmills Road. Mr Bell, the manager, lived near us. I can remember a time when, before electricity was installed, our house was lit by gas. The delicate little globes that looked as if they were made of fine lace gave off a bright warm glow when illuminated by the gas flame. The large quantities of coal used in the manufacture of gas were brought to Portrush by boat and it was a busy scene at the harbour when the cargo was being discharged and loaded onto horse-drawn carts and lorries.

I must mention another great plus about living in Causeway Street in those days in the mid-twentieth century – the old Causeway tram. For me it was the icing on the cake. It passed up and down the street several times a day on its way to and from the Causeway, more frequently in the summer months, and I can still recall the steely rumble of its coming and going. There was a tram stop practically outside our front door (our house was on the opposite side of the track) so we knew the timetable off by heart. The tram was equipped with a large bell, sounded by the driver to warn of its stopping and starting and to clear any obstructions on the track. Sometimes we took a family trip to the Causeway, nearly always choosing to sit in one of the open carriages and to us youngsters it always seemed like a great adventure.

> Although I did not know it at the time, a gentleman who had a very interesting link with the old trams was a Causeway Street man. Mr Samuel Bacon, who died in 1951 at the age of 83, had lived all his life in Portrush. His obituary stated: "At the age of 12, he began work with the Giant's Causeway Tramway Company, where his father was also employed, and assisted in the laying of the first tram lines. In later years he drove one of the steam trams which were in operation before the electric trams were introduced."

When he retired in 1935, Mr Bacon had chalked up forty years service with the Tramway Company. His wife had died some seventeen years earlier and surviving him were three sons and a daughter. One of his sons, Jack, was for many years Caddie Master at Royal Portrush and I remember interviewing him on one occasion for a golf-related feature I was researching. He was very knowledgeable about the game and had some great stories to tell.

So it was a sad day, particularly for the Bacon family, in 1949 when the old Causeway tram made its last run, leaving its mark on the pages of history and leaving Portrush very much the poorer for its passing.

THE HOUSE THAT FRED LIVED IN

Before we leave Causeway Street and its neat rows of houses, many of them three-storeys, its broad pavements and relatively traffic-free thoroughfare, I want to take you to one house in particular, Number 76, just a couple of doors up from what, in the 1950s, was the Palladium Ballroom. This is the house where Fred Daly lived when he was growing up in Portrush. So the future Open Champion lived not all that far from the golf course. It would have taken him less than ten minutes to walk from his front door to the Clubhouse. He learned his caddie skills from an early age and this must surely have ignited his passion for the game which he played with so much grace and skill throughout his trophy-studded career. The house now bears an Ulster History Circle Blue Plaque denoting its link with this famous golfing son of Portrush.

Not so long ago, as I was taking a walk, unashamedly nostalgic, along 'this happy highway' of Causeway Street, the words of a favourite poem, *The Land of Lost Content,* by AE Houseman, written in metaphorical language of great beauty, kept running through my head and seemed to sum up perfectly my feelings:

Into my heart an air that kills
From yon far country blows;
What are those blue remembered hills
What spires, what farms are those?

That is the land of lost content
I see it shining plain,
The happy highways where I went
And cannot come again.

CHAPTER 20

AN AMAZING CATCH

Holiday story with a twist

IN ANOTHER CHAPTER I alluded to my early journalistic training in the gathering of local news items for the *Chronicle's* weekly Portrush Notes column. I thought it would be nice to include some of these, (none of them written by me), selected at random from the 1951 archives because they do give a glimpse of life and times in Portrush at that period.

The first one is a real beauty and if it happened today it would definitely be a story that would not be out of place in any of the national dailies.

It's told under the heading 'Believe it or not' and concerns a young boy, Jack Shortt from Sheffield, who was spending a holiday in Portrush with his family. Apparently young Jack was very fond of outdoor sports and earlier in the week had gone for a swim at the East Strand.

After enjoying his swim and getting dressed, he decided to rinse the sand from his trunks and paddled into the sea to do so. The story continued:

> "He let the trunks fall into the water and could not recover them.
> Undeterred, he took to fishing the next day, and about 27 hours after
> the swimming incident was enjoying that patient sport off the Blue
> Pool rocks. His line tightened. He pulled it in. The 'catch' was a pair of
> swimming togs. Marks on the trunks showed they belonged to him."

Amazing. Today a story like that would be worthy of more extensive coverage and perhaps a photograph of the young boy proudly holding, in triumph, his catch – not a fish but a pair of swimming trunks!

I remember always keeping my ear to the ground for the off-beat or quirky little story and sometimes it did pay off, like this one about a 'birdie' – not the sort golfers like to get:

> "A few weeks ago a pair of mistle thrushes built their nest on the top
> of a wall dividing two residences in Morrison Park and attracted a lot

of attention in the neighbourhood. This was an unusual site because mistle thrushes favour trees for their home. Interested residents followed the family life of the thrushes from the nest-building stage until the last two of the four fledglings took off on Tuesday morning. The other two flew off earlier in the week. The mistle thrush is the largest of the thrush species (the redwing being the smallest). Another nature note from the same vicinity – a rabbit has been observed to have befriended an apparently homeless cat. Both share the same burrow. Seemingly cats as well as people are experiencing a shortage of living accommodation!"

Strangely, a few weeks later another story about a thrush was recorded. It stated:

"While leaving his work in the bus depot of the Ulster Transport Authority early one morning a local bus conductor saw a thrush 'plodding' along the pavement unable to fly because of tar on its wings and feet. Catching the thrush he returned home and gave it a 'margarine' bath. Within five minutes the thrush was airborne again to the accompaniment of excited chirpings as it sang its appreciation of the conductor's act of kindness."

MONKEY BUSINESS

It wouldn't happen today, but in the 1950s the question of wild animals in circuses and other places of entertainment was not such a burning issue. For instance, this little story could be found in the Portrush Notes column:

"Two chimpanzees, believed to be the most intelligent species of animal in the world, arrived at Barry's Amusements from Denmark during the week and will remain for the summer season. Young or old never seem to tire of watching the antics of these agile animals and the two in question – Trully and Felli – want to meet all the children as soon as possible."

SPECTACULAR FIRE DIVING

In those days diving displays were still popular, particularly at the Blue Pool. It was reported in the Notes column that one of these, in the summer of

1951, had attracted upwards of 2,000 spectators. This was the largest number recorded at this venue for a good many years. The Notes continued:

"A voluntary committee comprising Messrs D Wright, O'Hara Logan, GE Pepper, A Duke and GH McCann, organised the event. Taking part were Liam Jones (Wellington SC), the Irish Olympic choice, and his sister, Clare. They gave demonstrations of swimming. The divers – comic and straight – were: Ian Bamford, Hugh Patton, CC Mann, Jack Kyle and the Misses M McGraw, A Matheson, I and M Bruce. GE Pepper was announcer and commentator."

I remember attending some of these diving displays myself and nearly always the star of the show was Hughie Patton, one of the most dare-devil divers of the time. Often there were midnight diving displays and Hughie's speciality at these was a daring fire dive – wearing suitable attire, he would be set alight and then take a running dive off the high diving board into the churning water. It was spectacular and drew massive applause from the enthralled spectators.

However, he was not the only diver in Portrush who could perform this spectacular feat. Carl Chambers was equally daring and this next note about another floodlit diving display at the Blue Pool describes just how spectacular, and how dangerous, it was:

"The highlight of the evening was Carl Chambers' sensational fire dive. Carl was covered with petrol and when 'lit' he dived from the high board into the blazing petrol-covered pool."

The report lists others who took part in that display and I knew most of them: Jeanine McCandless, Amy Matheson, Ruth Matheson, Louise Trufelli, John Forster, John Thompson, Sam Fleming, Malachy Austin, Jerry Paul, Derek Wright, Ronnie McGeagh, B Fleming, Freddy Hunter (Belfast) and Raymond Lindsay (Belfast).

Members of the diving 'Crazy Gang' were listed as George McCann, O'Hara Logan, John Caithness, Ronnie Cameron, Alex Duke (Belfast) and Eddie Christie.

VICTOR SILVESTER

The main 'ballroom of romance' in Portrush for many years until the early part of the 1950s' was in the Barry's Amusements complex and very popular it was too. I remember the old dancing classes there – not formalised as such but anyone who went to the Thursday dances understood that they were largely for beginners. The idea was that a young chap like myself who wanted to learn a few steps could ask any girl he fancied and, assuming she was a seasoned dancer, she was expected to pass on a few tips to the aspiring Fred Astaire. The reverse also applied to girls, of course, although there were not too many Fred Astaires to call upon!

Anyway, I came across this little Portrush note from 1951 under the headline: 'Victor Silvester at Barry's':

"Barry's Ballroom was packed to capacity on Monday night when Victor Silvester's Ballroom Orchestra from the BBC Ballroom, London, was the main feature. This was the first appearance of the band in Northern Ireland. Mr WR Knox, chairman of the Urban Council, welcomed Mr Silvester and his Orchestra to the resort and complimented Mrs Trufelli on keeping the entertainment provided at the ballroom at such a high standard. Harry Blackwood and His Music Makers played at intervals with vocalist Leslie Mann. The winner of the tenth heat of the series in the Festival Girl competition in the ballroom on Saturday night was Miss Nancy McDowell, Arcorn Square. Harry Blackwood and His Music Makers supplied the music."

A PLEASANT SURPRISE FOR JOE LOSS

A couple of years later, Barry's Ballroom had closed and in its place was the newly-built Arcadia Ballroom, the 'ballroom by the sea' as it became known. It had an early visit from one of Britain's top ranking bands, Joe Loss and his Orchestra. The ballroom had a spectacular situation, right on the edge of the shore and played a key role in the resort's entertainment programme for many years. A sign of the changing times – Portrush has been without a ballroom for a good many years now.

The Portrush Notes column carried this item about the visit of Joe Loss and his Orchestra to the Arcadia Ballroom:

"The visit of the 'king of rhythm', Joe Loss to the Arcadia Ballroom on Tuesday night, attracted a large number of dancers from a wide area. The popular band-leader, whose orchestra has made many broadcasts and recordings, received an enthusiastic welcome, and the dancers were treated to his orchestra's arrangements of all the popular hit tunes of the moment.

"The singing stars with the orchestra, Rose Brennan ('Ireland's nightingale of song'), Larry Gretton and Ross McManus, were also accorded a great welcome. The resident band in the Arcadia, Dave Glover and his Show-Band, with Oliver Harcourt (broadcasting vocalist) were present as relief band and fully merited the praise given by Joe Loss himself before the close. Mr Loss also said that it was a pleasant surprise to find such a magnificent ballroom in Portrush and to meet such a wonderful audience."

CHAPTER 21

DRIVING OFF INTO HISTORY

Rapturous welcome for a local hero

I T MUST HAVE BEEN an intensely proud moment for Fred Daly, standing on the first tee at Royal Portrush to begin his opening round in the 1951 Open Golf Championship. Born and bred in Portrush, he had learned his golfing skills on these testing fairways. This was where he had caddied as a young boy, where he had felt the first stirrings of an ambition that perhaps one day he could become a professional golfer.

He had already brought a large slice of golfing honour and glory to his home town four years earlier by winning The Open, most coveted of golf titles, the first Ulsterman to do so, a record that stood until Darren Clarke's great victory in 2011.

'Freddie,' as he was known to everyone in Portrush, was indeed a local hero and one can only imagine his thoughts and feelings on that momentous day in the summer of 1951 on the first tee, the local boy whose dream had come true. He was now regarded as one of the world's foremost golfers. He was living his dream.

The memory of his tremendous 1947 win at Hoylake would no doubt have given him a huge confidence boost. Now, on his home turf, although up against some of the most talented players in the game, he would not have been intimidated. He had already shown that he could hold his own with the best of them. He knew the Dunluce links like the back of his hand. He would have relished the challenge and, as a former champion, was more than ready to take it on.

Following his triumphant win at Hoylake in 1947, he had been given a great welcome when he arrived in Portrush, his name carved on the coveted Claret Jug. A good chunk of the population, some 3,000 people, gathered outside the Town Hall where he was given a civic reception and where he was hailed as the town's 'conquering hero.'

The Urban Council chairman, Mr WR Knox, said they had watched

Fred's progress in the golfing world with pride and pleasure and his latest achievement had brought great delight to everyone in the town and throughout the Province. His latest success in winning The Open reflected the greatest credit on his prowess as a golfer and on Portrush, his native town, which was justly renowned for its golf and famous golfers.

The chairman went on to recall the days when, as a boy, Fred was always keen on golf. Everyone in the town and district, he said, had followed his career with interest, and his winning of The Open had given great pleasure to all. It had even been the inspiration for a sermon in the Presbyterian Church!

Perhaps the text of the sermon had something to do with his next comment:

"One thing we admire about Fred more than anything else is that success has not gone to his head. He is just the same smiling, genial, unassuming friend we knew as a boy. That quality has endeared him to everybody and long may he continue to be so."

Fred Daly, of course, was professional at the Balmoral Club and in reference to this, Mr Knox said the Club had done a great deal to help him and had every reason to be proud of their professional. He concluded:

"The people of Portrush are always willing to do anything to help Fred in his distinguished career and we all wish him God speed and great happiness no matter where his career might take him."

At the same function, the Captain of Royal Portrush Club, Lieut-Colonel CO Hezlet, described Fred's performance at Hoylake as 'magnificent.' He was a most worthy winner, adding:

"We all know what a great sportsman Fred is and what fame he has brought to Portrush. He was brought up and learned his golf in Portrush."

GREATEST OF ALL GOOD GOLFERS
PRODUCED BY PORTRUSH

He paid tribute to Fred's sportsmanlike gesture in competing in the Irish Open Championship after his strenuous week at Hoylake when he could have done with a rest. He was a big attraction at the Championship and his appearance had helped the receipts tremendously.

Interestingly, Colonel Hezlet revealed that the Royal Portrush Club was endeavouring to have The Open Championship played at Portrush for the first time in Ireland. They had one of the finest courses possible for the major tournament and all the necessary facilities.

The Colonel concluded by describing Fred Daly as "the greatest of all the good golfers produced by Portrush."

Another speaker, Mr Harry Porter, past Captain of Balmoral Club, who was present at the Championship at Hoylake, said that if Ulster had ever had a better ambassador playing in England than Fred Daly he would like to meet him. Balmoral Club, he said, took credit for recognising Fred's great capabilities long before anybody else seemed to do so and had given him the opportunity he needed to reach the top of the golfing tree.

With typical modesty, Fred replied that he was glad to be back in his native town of Portrush after winning The Open. He thanked the people for the warmth of their welcome and the council for honouring him with a civic reception. He acknowledged the help and encouragement he had received from a local businessman, RA Chalmers, in his early career.

The last word at that civic reception was from Mr Chalmers, who said that eighteen years ago he had recognised in Daly a potential champion. Fred might travel far abroad in future, but he hoped he would never forget the love they had for him in Portrush.

Many more fine tributes of a similar nature awaited Fred Daly, 'the conquering hero,' at the Royal Portrush Clubhouse where he was given a rapturous welcome.

Fred Daly had won the title at Hoylake in 1947 with rounds of 73, 70, 78 and 72. He was runner-up in 1948, third in 1950 and 1952 and fourth in 1951. He won the Ulster Championship twelve times and was the winner of the Irish Open in 1946. He was made an honorary member of the Royal Portrush Club in June of that year.

Fred Daly was given a great send-off by friends and well-wishers as he boarded the Liverpool boat on his homeward journey after winning The Open in 1947. Among them was Max Faulkner who would win the title in Fred's home town of Portrush when The Open was played over the Dunluce links in 1951.

CHAPTER 22

MANY HAPPY RETURNS FOR MAX

It was a nice angle to the story

ACCORDING TO A REPORT in the *Pittsburg Gazette*, supplied by the Associated Press correspondent covering the 1951 Open Championship in Portrush, the secret of Max Faulkner's victory was down, at least in part, to an unusual exercise he had been doing. The opening paragraph explained all:

> "Methodical Max Faulkner, a par-wrecking Englishman who spent one winter milking cows to strengthen his golfing hands, won the British Open Golf Championship today in a dramatic rain-soaked finish".

I don't remember hearing about that milking slant on the story or having read about it in any of the local newspapers at the time but perhaps the Associated Press reporter had inside information. Anyway, it was a nice angle to the story of a great win.

The *Coleraine Chronicle*, which may have had one of its own reporters covering the Championship, picked up on the amazing shot the winner pulled off at the 16th hole in the third round.

> "His drive had been pulled to the left and – this was a real piece of fortune – the ball bounced obligingly off the fence onto the fairway. Nevertheless he was cramped for his second and after several practice swings decided to take the bull by the horns and use a wood, despite the strong wind blowing from the left. He reached the green and putted 'dead' for his four."

Unfortunately, I was not there to see that fantastic shot. His playing partner, the American Frank Stranahan, said afterwards that it was the finest golf shot he had ever seen.

At that stage Faulkner was leading the field by four shots. He had hooked his tee shot and the ball had landed dangerously close to an out-of-bounds fence. He had a difficult choice to make: he could either chip the ball safely onto the fairway and almost certainly end up dropping a shot. Or, with a three wood, he could take a full swing, flighting the ball out of bounds but with sufficient fade to hopefully bring it back into play, a daunting shot for even the most fearless of players. This is how another reporter described what happened next:

> "Reaching for his three wood, Faulkner lashed the ball over the fence and, as the gallery watched spellbound, the ball dutifully turned right, right and right again as it crossed the fence and bounded up the fairway onto the green."

I'm sure the applause from the gallery would have been deafening. They had just witnessed what was undoubtedly the shot of the Championship.

In my mind's eye I can still see this stylish player striding up and down the fairways in the brightly coloured outfits he wore, usually a combination of yellow and orange and red. Even to my inexpert eye he seemed a supremely confident player.

Max Faulkner had started the last round leading by six strokes and finished two ahead of his nearest rival, Antonio Cerda. For a time it had looked as if Cerda, from Argentina, who had been going well, might force a play-off but his hopes were dashed at the 16th hole. His drive had landed close to some steps near a barbed-wire fence leaving a very difficult shot. He had to settle for a six – and Max was home and dry.

So 1951 was Max Faulkner's year, the year he made his mark by winning the world's most prestigious golf championship and he did it in Portrush. His name is carved with pride in the annals of the Royal Portrush Club; many people believe that he helped put the seaside town that much more firmly on the golfing map. I'm sure it marked a turning point of some kind or another with regard to golf tourism in the local area. For a good while afterwards the Club and the town basked in the glory of The Open.

Perhaps the Englishman had a slight advantage – apart from milking cows, that is – because he would have been familiar with the twists and turns of the Dunluce links. At the prize ceremony following his great victory, he reminded his audience that he had played at Portrush twice before – on both occasions in the Irish Open. In 1938, at the age of 21, he finished third and in 1947 he was again third.

He was overcome slightly by a little bit of nostalgia because he also recalled his boyhood days when, at the age of just 12, he had won his first competition, playing off a handicap of 16 and without receiving any strokes. At that time, he said, his ambition was to be Open Champion and a Ryder Cup player.

The trophy was presented to him by Brigadier GNC Martin, Captain of the Royal Portrush Club. Colonel CO Hezlet, a former Captain of the Club, also spoke and referred to the fact that it was the first time the event had been held outside Great Britain. It had been, he said, a tremendous success and the Royal and Ancient were "very glad that they had held the event in Northern Ireland."

For the record, the leading scores were: Max Faulkner (Unattached) 71, 70, 70, 74 – 285; A Cerda (Argentina) 74, 72, 71, 70 – 287; CH Ward (Little Aston) 76, 72, 74, 68 – 290; F Daly (Balmoral) 74, 70, 75, 78 – 292; J Adams (Wentworth) 68, 77, 75, 72 – 292; Bobby Locke (South Africa) 71, 74, 74, 74 – 293; Bill Shankland (Australia) 73, 76, 72, 72 – 293; Norman Sutton (England) 73, 70, 74, 76 – 293; Peter Thompson (Australia) 70, 75, 73, 75 – 293; Harry Weetman (England) 73, 71, 75, 74 – 293.

It was estimated that some 5,000 spectators had been on the course for most of the final day's play, including the then Governor of Northern Ireland, Vice Admiral Earl Granville.

In 2001, on the 50th anniversary of his Open triumph at Royal Portrush, Max Faulkner was honoured with an OBE for services to golf. He died in 2005 at the age of 88.

Max Faulkner was not attached to any club at the time of his Open success. He completed the four rounds in a total of 285 strokes, eight ahead of his old rival and holder of the title for the previous two years, Bobby Locke, the defending champion, from South Africa, who finished tied for sixth place. Had Locke won at Portrush that year he would have become the first player since 1882 to win the title for the third consecutive year, but on the Dunluce links, for whatever reason, the verdict of one correspondent was that he had "never played the golf of a champion."

Another English player, Charlie Ward, took third place on 290. Local hero Fred Daly, trying to replicate his tremendous win at Hoylake in 1947, had to settle for a share of fourth place with Jimmy Adams from Scotland on 292.

Faulkner's touch around the greens throughout that 1951 Championship was magical and played big part in his success. One leading commentator observed: "What made him a winner that week was his fantastic touch on the greens." He was believed to have acquired some 300 putters over the years and was always searching for the perfect one. He was recognised also as "a superb striker of the ball."

Huge crowds had followed the ups and downs of the players over the three days and their behaviour had impressed one of the leading golf writers of the day. Frank Pennink wrote in *Golf Monthly*: "The intimate knowledge of the game shown by the enthusing Irish multitudes was another pleasant feature of The Open. They were well controlled, and who will blame them if their loudest applause was reserved for their own heroes, Daly, Bradshaw and O'Connor. I imagine there must have been some 7,000 to 8,000 of them on the last day. Therefore a financial success must have been assured, most welcome and essential nowadays."

In fact, the attendance receipts for the week of The Open amounted to £4,000. Commander JA Storer Carson was upbeat. The attendance figures, he said, were "well up to the average for the Championship." He went on to pay a glowing tribute to the Royal Portrush Club: "The arrangements were excellent. Nothing was left undone. The greens, tees and fairways were perfect and the crowd control was first class. I never in all my experience saw such well behaved galleries." It was estimated that the total attendance was between 10,000 and 12,000 with about 6,000 to 7,000 on the final day.

> "It was all I ever wanted. Winning The Open meant everything to me."
>
> Max Faulkner

Max Faulkner and Christy O'Connor senior, met up again in Portrush in 1995 at the British Senior Championship – O'Connor, one of Ireland's most successful golfers, had also played in the 1951 Open and now aged 70, was again competing on the Dunluce links – he had already won the Senior title on several occasions.

For Max Faulkner, it was more of a family occasion this time round. He was back in Portrush to support his son-in-law, Brian Barnes, who was making his debut in the Senior event. And it turned out to be a winning debut.

CHAPTER 23

CATCHING THE BUS – AND THE LAST JAUNTING-CAR

A little bit of transport history

SOME INTERESTING STATISTICS RELATING to public transport in Portrush in the middle of the twentieth century emerged with the opening of a new bus terminal in a central part of the town. It was brought fully into operation in June, 1951 and this is how the structure was described in a press report of the opening:

> "Of attractive design, the Portrush terminal is adjacent to the railway station and occupies the site of the old pleasure gardens opposite Kerr Street. Work, which was started last Autumn, will not be completed until this Autumn when a pre-cast shelter will be erected on the 250 foot long main platform beside the present temporary inquiry kiosk and inspectors' office."

The terminal had been built over an old railway track leading to the harbour and was one of a number which the Ulster Transport Authority was planning to build throughout the country "in an effort to meet urgent needs" and for the safety and convenience of the travelling public.

The Portrush terminal was badly needed even though there was some criticism about its design and location. It would, nevertheless, provide accommodation for 69 buses and would be "a boon to the resort" from where 123 buses arrived and departed daily from and to Portstewart and Coleraine in addition to numerous long distance vehicles and upwards of 30 to and from the Giant's Causeway, Ballycastle and Bushmills.

The main platform, surrounded by a concrete road of 1,330 square yards, would be used for these service vehicles and another platform, 160 feet long and surrounded by 3,600 square yards of tar macadam surface roadway, would be mainly used for excursion and special tour vehicles.

A press release gave this added information:

"During last summer, as many as 60 private hire buses arrived daily and this number, which was almost double the previous year's figure, is rapidly increasing. Since the private hire service was resumed after the war, the number of vehicles has shown a big increase each year."

The design of the new terminal was somewhat futuristic. Triangular in shape, with sides 400 feet, 380 feet and 240 feet long, the whole area had required some 5,000 tons of filling.

At a subsequent press reception, the Transport Authority's passenger manager, Mr REM Hughes, said the terminal filled a long-felt want in Portrush and added greatly to the safety and convenience of the public. The Authority was also alive to the comfort of their employees, the terminal including rest-room accommodation for the staff.

There were mixed views in Portrush about its design and location. Local councillors described it as "an eyesore on the finest patch of ground in Portrush"; "a repellent, ugly and idiotic monstrosity"; "a waste of public money…"

However, the new bus terminal at the top of Kerr Street, just opposite the Town Hall, long since removed, served its purpose for a good many years. I used it many times myself and never heard anyone complaining about it. Perhaps Portrush was ahead of its time when it came to bus terminals.

The area around the Station Square and the former site of the old terminal has been refurbished in recent times and restored to something of its former glory, part of an overall regeneration plan for the resort.

END OF AN ERA

This was also the general area where the once popular jaunting-cars would park up waiting for hire. In 1951 they had all but vanished from the streets but one or two could still be seen and were still a novelty attraction.

Their history in Portrush is interesting. In summer they were a popular mode of transport. Most of the drivers, or jarveys, took great pride in their cars and horses. An insight into just how particular they were was revealed at the start of each summer when about forty or fifty of them would line up for an impressive parade and inspection. This was required by the town council which issued licences for the vehicles on an annual basis.

This, from an old report, is how the inspection was carried out:

"Upwards of forty magnificently equipped cars were drawn up in line in Mark Street, a display which, it is doubtful, could be equalled anywhere in Ireland. The teams proved eminently satisfactory, and having made a circuit of the town, they were again drawn up in front of the Town Hall, when Mr RH Gilmore, MRCVS, Coleraine and Mr W Gill, Cromore, again inspected them with a view to allocating prizes presented by the council for the best equipped teams."

The last jaunting-car to ply for hire on the summer streets of Portrush probably slipped quietly into history in the early 1950s, bringing to an end another small chapter in the resort's seaside story.

They took great pride in their cars and horses.

CHAPTER 24

RUN RABBIT RUN, RUN, RUN…

"… they would hardly have been able to snatch balls from the greens."

WHEN IT WAS LEARNED that the 1951 Open Championship was to be played at Royal Portrush there was understandable delight in the North Coast resort – but it was bad news for rabbits! Apparently those furry little pests had been causing havoc on the Dunluce links, so much so that drastic measures, which included the use of gas and poison, had to be used to control them.

At the Club's annual meeting in June, 1950, Club members were urged to devote "an occasional afternoon" throughout the winter months to the task of destroying the rabbits. According to one member, apparently speaking from experience, the best way of doing this was "getting at them" with poison and gas. So presumably volunteers would have been issued with appropriate quantities of those lethal substances before setting out on their grisly task.

I wonder what sort of problems the rabbits were causing to provoke such draconian measures. Unlike foxes, they would hardly have been able to snatch balls from the greens and run off with them. I wonder, too, how many, if any, of the members volunteered their extermination services.

As far as I know, not a trace of a rabbit was to be found anywhere during The Open Championship. I certainly didn't see any and I was there as a spectator to witness a lot of the play. At any rate, they would probably have been keeping a low profile during the actual Championship – they would not have been happy with such huge crowds of people invading their territory.

It was the first time The Open Championship had been played on a course outside the British mainland, so a large slice of golfing history was made. Now, six decades later, hopes are high that history might repeat itself on the Royal Portrush links. Those hopes will surely have been boosted considerably with the successful staging of the Irish Open Championship in 2012.

I was a ticket-holding spectator every day of that Championship but in 1951, as a young boy growing up in Portrush, I must admit to sneaking on and off the course, melting into the crowds of spectators, managing to keep out of the way of stewards and enjoying quite a bit of the play in that historic event.

Incidentally, those Royal Portrush bunnies don't seem to have posed much of a problem for the great Fred Daly, playing on his home course and the winner in 1947. He gave a good account of himself and finished in joint fourth place.

To be fair, it wasn't only rabbits on the agenda at that 1950 meeting. The condition of the Clubhouse was also giving some cause for concern. It was reported:

> "In an effort to put the Clubhouse in as good condition as reasonably possible for staging The Open Championship, a special general meeting was held at which it was agreed to spend £2,500 on vital repairs and re-decoration and improvement work."

The Club's finances were "sufficiently buoyant" to stand the cost of the scheme. Finally, the Club appealed for volunteers who could guarantee to give 100 per cent of their time during the Championship week to do "all sorts of jobs." They needed a lot of people both part-time and full-time.

The 1951 Championship was a triumph for the Royal Portrush Club in terms of the smoothness and efficiency of the organisation. The winner, of course, was the flamboyant English player, Max Faulkner. I had the privilege of seeing him sink his final putt on the eighteenth green. I don't remember if it was a birdie. But I do know there wasn't a rabbit in sight!

SNAKES IN THE GRASS

Meeting a rabbit on the golf course isn't the worst thing that could happen to a player, but what about snakes? That was something Fred Daly had to look out for earlier in 1951 when he captained a British professional golf team which toured extensively, and successfully, in South Africa. In April of that year, following an absence of some four months, the Balmoral professional returned to Belfast "sun-tanned and looking fit."

Interviewed by a local reporter, he said he had travelled about 25,000 miles and, during the last eight weeks of the tour, the British golfers played almost every day. He had found it difficult to become accustomed to the heat.

He was asked about the difference between golf as played in Northern Ireland and in South Africa. He explained:

"Perhaps the most important difference is that when a ball goes into the rough, as in Ulster, the idea is to get out again as quickly as possible, but South African golfers have the danger of poisonous snakes as an added incentive."

He had not seen any snakes himself, adding "at least that is something you don't have to worry about at Portrush."

Another observation was the length they were able to drive the ball in South Africa and he gave this example: "At Bethlehem, between Cape Town and Johannesburg, I took a five-iron to get onto the green 190 yards away. My shot landed on the green and then went yards over. Harry Bradshaw took a six-iron and went even farther. This sort of thing is very likely to happen in South Africa where the air is so different from home."

That British tour which Fred Daly led was very successful, the team winning four of the five "Tests" with sides representing South Africa.

FRED'S TOOTHACHE CURE

Just a couple of weeks before he was due to compete in the 1951 Open in his home town of Portrush, Fred had to deal with a hazard of another kind on the golf course, one not encountered too often by many golfers. Fortunately, he was not competing in a major tournament when he was struck by a bout of toothache.

The Ryder Cup golfer and former Open champion, was playing in a prestigious 36-hole exhibition match at Letchworth (Hertfordshire). He decided that trying to play golf with a nagging toothache was not a good idea and during a break for lunch, came up with a solution.

"So he had the tooth taken out on the course at lunchtime," was how one golf reporter put it. He continued: "Then, partnered by Dai Rees, he went on to beat Australians Norman von Nida and Bill Shankland."

It was probably the only time in the history of professional golf that a dentist had to be summoned to the course to deal with a player's toothache.

That extraction, performed not on the actual course, presumably, but in the Clubhouse, did the trick for Fred because in the afternoon he carded a round of 65, beating the 20-year-old course record by three shots.

That record-breaking round must have given him a good feeling about his chances in The Open just a couple of weeks ahead. But alas his hopes of winning the title again, this time in his home town of Portrush, were not to be, although he did acquit himself well, finishing in fourth place.

Norman Sutton (Leigh) found himself "down to the wire" quite literally speaking when calling for a ruling into the playability of his second shot in one of his rounds in the 1951 Open. His second shot at the 18th hole had finished underneath a wire-bound fence and "a solemn R and A Committee carried out an inspection." They ruled that the ball was in bounds – by one quarter of an inch so they must have had to get out the tape measure. The ball could not be played because of the fence and he was permitted to drop it without penalty two club lengths away. His pitch landed on the green and he putted out for a five.

CHAPTER 25

HYPNOTIC APPEAL OF PORTRUSH

...the first time anything like this had been done in Ireland

A N UNUSUAL LITTLE EXPERIMENT in hypnotism was successfully completed in Portrush back in 1951 when a man in the town was hypnotised over the telephone from Belfast. It was believed to be the first time anything like this had been done in Ireland and it was, apparently, very well authenticated.

The Majestic Cinema was the venue at the Portrush end and the Belfast link was the Grand Central Hotel. The hypnotist there was a gentleman called Harry Simons, described as a 34-year-old London company director while 28-year-old John McCaw was the 'guinea pig' in Portrush.

Reporting on the experiment, the *Northern Constitution* stated:

> "Mr McCaw 'went over' within a few seconds of speaking to Mr Simons, and during the 27 minutes he was under the spell, as a result of suggestions, he laughed heartily and sang a song. On awakening, Mr McCaw carried out a post-suggestion and shouted 'Whoopee.'"

While he was in a state of hypnosis, the *Constitution* reporter, and two others, Captain WR Shutt, Sports and Entertainments Officer and Councillor J McLean, were challenged to try and awaken Mr McCaw, "but he was in such a deep sleep that their efforts were useless." At the Belfast end the demonstration was witnessed by members of the hotel staff, two reporters and a number of guests. The *Constitution* report continued:

> "When Mr McCaw returned to full consciousness he said that he remembered nothing after Mr Simons had snapped his fingers and could give no explanation as to why he should choose to sing 'Rainbows.' He felt no ill-effects as a result of the experiment and was 'simply great!'"

There was more to come. While under hypnosis it had been suggested to Mr McCaw that next morning at precisely 11.30 am he would telephone an advertisement to two Belfast newspapers from the office of the Majestic Cinema. "This he did exactly at the time stated, and did not know why he did so," the *Constitution* report confirmed.

Mr McCaw was an interesting subject. An ex-fighter pilot, he suffered from a back injury following a plane crash in North Africa. For more than two years he suffered chronically from insomnia but after treatment from Mr Simons had experienced refreshing sleep each night, so it was reported.

Some of the background of Mr Simons, who was on a business trip to Northern Ireland, was also given in that old report. He had studied the science of hypnotism as a hobby after seeing it used as therapeutic treatment by a French psychiatrist in a military hospital at Basingstoke where he had been a patient for two and a half years as a result of an accident while he was serving with the Royal Army Service Corps. He now performed only for charitable purposes, mainly for St Dunstan's. He had been booked to give a performance in Portrush in March in aid of British Legion funds.

The arrangements for the telephone demonstration were made by Mr EJ Dineen, manager of the Majestic Cinema, Portrush, assisted by Mr A Jones, Belfast. Telephone arrangements at the Portrush end were carried out by Mr RS Ross, Supervisor, Coleraine Telephone Exchange.

I found myself wondering what sort of advertisement Mr McCaw would have placed in those two Belfast newspapers. Perhaps something to do with the hypnotic appeal of Portrush!

CHAPTER 26

ROAD RACING HISTORY WAS MADE IN 1951

Historic year for North-West 200

IN MAY EACH YEAR, a big event in the Portrush sporting calendar is the North-West 200 motor-cycle road race but in 1951 it was record-breaking on several fronts and not only among the riders. For the first time 'foreign riders' were to be seen on the famous Coleraine, Portrush, Portstewart circuit. Also it was the first time in road racing history that an Irish event had been staged over two days – an innovation that was followed by the Ulster Grand Prix. According to a news report, the total insurance cover amounted to £50 million and was a world record for any sport. The report continued:

> "In finance too it is record-breaking. The first race in 1929 cost about £250 to promote; today's costs are slightly over £3,500. To the man-in-the-street the sum seems staggering and unbelievable, but it is quite a true figure and one which has given the organisers many months of work and worry".

It was pointed out that the competitors paid an entrance fee of £10 10s for two races and for this sum they received free hotel accommodation for four days, free insurance, free garage accommodation, plus free petrol and oil for race and practice so the promoters had "little income from each fee."

However, the North-West is a magnet each year for thousands of spectators and bike fans and undoubtedly today's costs with regard to the running of the event are equally as staggering as those quoted for 1951.

Joey Dunlop was not around then but the big name in road racing at the time was an English rider, Geoff Duke from St Helen's and he lived up to his reputation in that 1951 race. Riding a works Norton, he completed the course in a record-breaking average speed of 88.71 miles per hour. This broke the record set by another class rider, Artie Bell. He had set the record at 85.72 miles per hour the previous year.

In the tenth lap, Duke had set another record; he clocked "an amazing" speed of 92.27 miles per hour, thus becoming the first man to lap the circuit at over 90 miles per hour.

FIREWORKS REVIVAL

Fireworks displays were still an important part of the holiday entertainment programme in Portrush in the early 1950s, attracting thousands of spectators, converging mainly on Ramore Head, overlooking the Recreation Grounds, which were the best vantage point.

The displays had been abandoned during the war years and were revived in the summer of 1946 with a spectacular show attracting a record attendance of just over 14,000. The cost of the half-hour display, part of pageant which lasted over three hours, was something like £5 a minute.

The entertainment involved military bands and formation marching displays, community and choral singing. A report of that historic display concluded:

> "...the highlight of the pageant was the fireworks display which was well up to pre-war standards. The audience saw a vivid display with a galaxy of rockets and aerial artistry and ground set pieces. There was an impressive finale to the pageant. The military and pipe bands massed in the floodlit arena accompanying the Londonderriares Choir who sang the evening hymn after which the great audience rendered the National Anthem while a fireworks portrait of the King glowed in the background."

Such an attraction was that particular pageant and fireworks display that "...vast numbers thronged the streets of the town long before the start of the display."

ALL THE FUN OF THE BIG TOP

Before, during and after The Open Championship, there was no lack of holiday entertainment in Portrush and one of the biggest attractions was when the circus came to town. In Portrush that usually meant Duffy's Circus. For many years it came for two days in July and the crowds flocked to the Big Top.

John Duffy and Sons toured much of the Province with their 'People's

Circus,' described in press advertisements as "an Irish show for Irish people" and, for good measure, "The greatest show on Irish soil."

The circus entourage included a range of side-shows and a zoo and these were almost as popular as the show itself. In 1951 Duffy's Circus was being billed as "the best ever presented in Ireland" with "the world's latest stupendous programme of strong, Continental flavour." According to an old press release, Messrs Duffy:

> "...have got together a wonderful collection of Continental performers, all of whom have thrilled audiences in many parts of the world with their skill and daring."

There was no outcry in those days about animals being used in circus acts and Duffy's had plenty of them, including lions, elephants, bears, baboons, dogs "and several other interesting animals." I remember going to the circus as a young boy and I think some of those other interesting animals could have been snakes.

The price of admission was not exorbitant, even then. Ringside seats were two shillings, reserved seats four shillings and arena seats five shillings. Children were admitted to ringside seats for one shilling and half that price to all other seats.

Down through the years many other circuses came to Portrush but Duffy's, I think, was the most popular. After Portrush the circus itinerary included Ballymoney, Ballymena, Carnlough, Larne, Whitehead, Carrickfergus, Ballyclare and Antrim.

THE STRATO GIRL

Also in the same week as The Open Championship was an unusual 'sky high' attraction right in the centre of the town, courtesy of Barry's Amusements.

In the square just outside Barry's a huge 120 foot high pole had been erected and it gave rise to much speculation among visitors and residents alike as to just what was happening. The big attraction, it turned out, was 'The Strato Girl,' a Swedish aerial acrobat whose speciality was performing amazing feats atop this giant pole, and she gave daily performances for a week.

I remember seeing the Strato Girl in action and her performance was truly spectacular, stopping the traffic in the busy centre of Portrush with thousands of spectators – and some motorists – straining their necks to see her daring feats. A newspaper report explained:

"The Strato Girl is making her first appearance in Ireland. This is one of Barry's contributions to the town's Festival of Britain celebrations, and she thrilled her audiences with many breathtaking feats, including hand-stands executed at the top of the pole without safety appliances in blustering winds, which made balance more difficult."

A few days later, an early morning police patrol was surprised to spot, on top of the pole, a youth who had somehow managed to climb the dizzy height. He was persuaded to come down and when he reached the safety of terra firma, told the police that he had just wanted "to see what it was like at the top." No doubt he received a severe caution from the police and afterwards, stricter security was put in place to stop the like happening again.

The Strato Girl was just one of many novelty acts brought to Portrush by Barry's over the years. That Festival of Britain summer Barry's was also the venue for what was described as a Festival Hour for primary school pupils in the town, courtesy of the proprietors, Mr and Mrs Trufelli. Presumably it meant that for an hour the children could sample the considerable pleasures and delights of the amusement park free of charge.

In the same week between 500 and 600 pupils were also entertained by the management of one of the local cinemas, The Picture House, to a free film show. The film shown was "The National Barn Dance." Let's hope it was a bit more exciting to watch than its title would suggest!

VISIT OF DANISH OLYMPIC SWIMMERS

In the summer of 1951 members of the Danish Olympic swimming team visited Portrush and took part in a fascinating aquatic display at the harbour, an event which attracted upwards of 2,500 spectators. The programme included a variety of races and exhibition swimming. It was a charity event, funds going to the National Society for the Prevention of Cruelty to Children.

Here is an extract from a press report of the gala:

"Best performances were given by the Danish swimmers, Gerta Anderson, Olympic and European (1950) champion, who was outstanding in an exhibition of swimming and training methods;

Karl Ebbe, Danish breast-stroke champion and Sonja Jakadofsky and Neils Madsen of the tandem team."

The biggest applause, however, was not for the Danish team but was reserved for Leading Seaman JJ Magennis, VC, who, wearing a frogman's outfit, gave an outstanding display of expertise relating to a different set of aquatic skills.

Local swimmers had a chance to take part also, although not against the Olympic team! A 50 yard swimming race for juveniles resulted:

Girls – 1. Jeanene McCandless, 2. Amy Matheson, 3. Margaret Fleming.

Boys – 1. J Riddell, 2. P McAleese, 3. AJ Pollock.

Later the Danish team was officially welcomed to Portrush by the Council chairman, Mr WR Knox. In the evening they also attended a dance held in Barry's Ballroom, also in aid of NSPCC funds.

POINT-TO-POINT AT GLENVALE

The Route Hunt's annual Point-to-Point races at Glenvale, on the outskirts of Portrush, were still a big attraction at Easter in 1951 although for many years now the races have been taking place at Myroe, near Limavady.

That particular event was attended by about 10,000 spectators from all over Northern Ireland. There were good vantage points all around the course, especially in the vicinity of the paddock and finishing point. There were bookmakers in profusion, a "small army" of them and according to a press report the scene was "gay and colourful."

The report added: "The course, notwithstanding the inclement weather during the weekend, was in excellent order and while the runners were less numerous than had been anticipated, the racing on the whole was keen and particularly interesting."

There was one nasty incident, however. An accident occurred during the final race when Miss P Merrick's mount 'Are You Well' fell at the hospital fence. Miss Merrick, the only lady rider taking part, was thrown heavily and had to be rushed by ambulance to Ratheane Hospital in Coleraine where later she was stated to be 'fairly comfortable.'

CHAPTER 27

PRIZE FUND WAS THE BIGGEST EVER

Spectators can look forward to a grand week of golf

NOWADAYS, WINNERS OF ANY of the major golf tournaments can become millionaires overnight. That was certainly not the case back in 1951, although The Open did make a little bit of history when it was announced that the total prize-money on offer was £1,700, the largest ever.

That's a striking illustration of just how rich the competition has become today. The total prize fund on offer for the 2013 Championship, for example, was £5.25 million with a cheque for a cool £945,000 going to the winner. In 1951 the top prize for the winner was £300, the runner-up received £200, with £100, £75 and £50 for third, fourth and fifth places. There was also a cash prize for an additional ten players who qualified for the final day's play. In all, a total of 25 qualifiers would receive £20 each.

As a further incentive, with the aim of adding interest to the early rounds, a prize of £15 was on offer for the best score over 18 holes from Monday to Thursday. Another £15 was on offer for the player with the lowest aggregate score in the qualifying rounds played over the Portrush and Portstewart courses.

The organisers were probably expecting a big jump in the entry because of the increased prize-money but for whatever reason that was not the case. The entry of 180 was well below the figures for 1950 (262) and 1949 (246). One news report noted however:

> "The Open has always attracted top-flight players from all parts of the country and overseas, and with Bobby Locke making his effort to win the title for the third successive year, spectators can look forward to a grand week of golf which should satisfy the most ardent enthusiast."

GETTING A GRIP

Some of the top players were able to boost their earnings with endorsements of one kind or another, just like today, although not on such a lucrative scale.

In the official 1951 programme, for instance, Bobby Locke figured in two full page advertisements. One was for a range of Gradidge golf clubs by Slazenger with a close-up photograph illustrating the master's grip. The claim was that he had used this particular make of golf club throughout his career.

Mr Locke appeared again in another full page spread, this time triumphantly holding aloft the famous Claret Jug which, of course, he had won in 1949 and again in 1950. The advertisement was for the Dunlop '65' golf ball. Just how that ball got its '65' tag is interesting. Henry Cotton won three Open Championships. His round of 65 in the 1934 Open inspired the Dunlop golf company and the result was the famous Dunlop 65 golf ball.

Henry Cotton was quite a character. He is said to have had a penchant for bespoke tailored clothes. Two of his best known quotes are: "The best is always good enough for me," and "To be a champion you must act like one."

His name also figured prominently in the 1951 programme. It featured new Golf Master shoes by Saxone, designed by Cotton, who was described as Saxone's "Golf Shoe Designer and Chief Consultant." I suppose you could say there was a little twist of irony in this because Max Faulkner, who won the 1951 Championship, just happened to be wearing a pair of Saxone golf shoes. I wonder if they were the ones designed by Henry Cotton!

Another popular player, Dai Rees, described as "Britain's Golfer of the Year," was the big name used in an advertisement for the range of Penfold 'peri-dot' golf balls.

Away from the course – and commerce – some of the players found time to relax and enjoy themselves in the holiday entertainment on offer in Portrush during Open week. Bobby Locke, the defending champion, attended a special performance put on in the Town Hall by members of the Portrush Players and the Portrush Music Society.

It was judged to be a "very pleasing" entertainment and it is worth mentioning some of the cast, which included Ann Rawlings, Jim McNicholl, Fred Smythe, Maureen Cunningham, Isa Hawley, Gertrude Trimble, Joan Watson, Jim Hall, John Hickey and O'Hara Logan. Other members of the group taking part were Kathleen Black, Valerie Black, Dot Faulkner, Kathleen Gordon, Eleanor Killen, Etta Mottram-Gray, Avis Mulholland, Kathleen McCulloch, Honor O'Kane, Bertha Platt, Louis Bamford, Bill Hartley and Eli Lucas.

CHAPTER 28

ICONIC HOLE AT ANCIENT
GATEWAY OF ULSTER

It's a view much favoured by painters and photographers

ONE OF THE MOST scenic holes on the Championship Dunluce links at Royal Portrush is the sixth. Particularly from the green, the view, both seascape and landscape, with the Causeway headland its spectacular guardian, is hard to beat. No wonder this part of the northern coastline has been described as "an ancient gateway of Ulster."

It is a view much favoured by painters and photographers down through the years and has been featured in magazines and journals across the world and of course more recently in film and television productions, notably the hugely successful *Game of Thrones*.

Perhaps the most celebrated painting of the scene is the one that adorns a wall in the Royal Portrush Clubhouse and the cover of this book. A beautiful and much admired original, it is by Norman Wilkinson, an artist noted for his marine studies. The painting was commissioned by the LMS/NCC railway company and the image was used to produce a travel poster for the specific purpose of promoting rail links to Portrush.

It is one of a series of paintings by the same artist illustrating the many different sports and pastimes to be enjoyed within the areas covered by the LMS railway. Wilkinson, who studied at the Portsmouth and Southsea Schools of Art, also produced paintings for posters of Portstewart and the Giant's Causeway, promoting tourism generally, as well as for a range of Ulster and Ireland posters.

His original painting of the famous sixth hole at Royal Portrush was presented to the Club in 1950 by the then chairman of British Rail, Sir Eustace Missenden.

So it was not too surprising that when Prince Andrew officially opened the newly renovated and extended Clubhouse in 1990, he was presented with a painting of this most picturesque part of the course and coastline as a memento of the occasion. I'm sure the Prince would have recognised the splendid Causeway headlands and hopefully someone would have given him a brief outline of the chequered history of Dunluce Castle and those gleaming white cliffs – the White Rocks – with their many fascinating caves and inlets.

ANOTHER FAMOUS PAINTING

Recently I came across another very interesting painting of this scene, a small watercolour by George C Nash, at one time Secretary of the Royal Portrush Club, who was also well-known as a painter and author, probably more so as an author. One of his best known books is *Letters to the Secretary of a Golf Club*. His painting, from 1942, was sold at an auction in Bonham's in London in 2011 for £480. There's more about Mr Nash and his Portrush connection in another section of the book.

Here I will mention my own attachment to this famous golf hole. It is one of my favourite views and one I have painted a few times myself, including the version in one of the picture sections of this book. Also featured on an inside page is one of my pen and ink sketches based on Norman Wilkinson's painting.

In the early 1980s this iconic golf hole faced a serious threat from coastal erosion, so much so that an expensive scheme to combat the problem had to be carried out. An appeal was launched to raise funds for the project and the work was successfully completed. However, the erosion along this volatile part of the coastline is an ever present threat and now, it seems, it is likely that more protective measures will have to be undertaken.

The April 2014 edition of the Club's newsletter, *Royal Times* reported:

> "Erosion of the sand dune to the rear of the fifth green and sixth tee complex occurred during the winter months, brought about by a combination of high tides and heavy sea conditions. Council has taken some preliminary expert advice on the erosion, and whilst the consensus is that there will be sand replenishment during the summer months, there is likely to be a requirement for additional protection measures to be put in place. Further advice is being sought on the matter."

CHAPTER 29

PORTSTEWART'S OPEN WELCOME

Qualifying for high honours

Portstewart had high hopes that after 1951, although already well-known for the quality of its golf, it would become better known still, not only among those who came to watch, but also among those famous stars who would be competing.

An article in the 1951 official programme gave this assurance:

"Portstewart will welcome all these new friends – as well as old ones who have returned – warmly, for it has that friendly atmosphere which makes the stranger feel at home."

The Club had a distinguished history but at that point in time it was felt that its highest honour was still to come with its choice as a qualifying course for The Open Championship of 1951.

It was of this course that an old scribe, in the early part of the last century, beautifully wrote:

"…in the depths of their hearts [golfers] may know that they go to the wind-blown spaces in search of beauty and to hear the old music that has been played there for a million years – the lark's song, the sound of the waves, the curlew's call, the plover's fluke, and inhale an air that is at once redolent of the mountain and the sea, the fragrance of flowers, and the faint, piquant incense of a thousand turf fires in the mountain homes across the valley of the Bann."

OCEAN, MOUNTAIN AND RIVER VIEWS

The year 1909 marked a milestone in the history of golf in Portstewart with the official opening of a new golf course in the summer of that year. It was announced in the local press:

"The new 18-hole golf course west of the town which is now vying for popular favour with Portrush links on the one hand and Castlerock on the other, will be formally opened for play on Thursday next."

Beautifully sited, the course had uninterrupted views of ocean, mountain and river. A big turn-out was expected for the ceremony, to be followed by an exhibition match between James Edmundson of Bangor, a former Irish Open champion and Charles H Mayo of Burhill, another well-known professional of the day. A poster advertising the match proclaimed:

> "Both players are among the cleverest of the young school of professionals and the meeting is one that is sure to give rise to a good deal of interest in golfing circles."

Ten years later, a party of golf correspondents visited Portstewart shortly after some major works had been completed to improve the course and one of them was so impressed that he wrote, "there are those who declare that it is now one of the finest in Ireland."

BOOST FOR BUSINESS

The course was well used by residents and visitors alike and undoubtedly it gave an added boost to Portstewart as a holiday destination. A press report of the time had this comment:

> "It would be an interesting calculation to work out the exact sum in hard cash which the business people of Portstewart have derived as a result."

In the summer of 1913 it was noted that the popularity of Portstewart as a seaside resort continued to grow and that golfing was the chief recreation among a large portion of the holidaymakers. In fact, so many had been playing on the new links that a certain amount of congestion was being experienced. As an illustration of this, an interesting statistic was quoted:

> "When almost £100 was received in visitors' fees during the first seven days of the month (August), an idea of the popularity of the course may be gathered. A liberal sprinkling of players is also to be seen daily on the old links. Both courses are in capital order."

It was back in 1895 that the game of golf began to be taken seriously in Portstewart which at that time, according to one source, "has lagged behind in the race for popularity among northern watering-places." In a newspaper article published in May of that year, it was stated that Portstewart:

> "…has been regarded as an old fashioned Derry village, nestling quietly and quaintly by the seashore, beyond the sound of the rushing railway train. Time was when Portstewart could hold its head above any seaside resort in the North; but by a much regretted misfortune the railway was not allowed to approach the old place, and from this untoward circumstance its prosperity has to a large extent been retarded."

So golf and its growing popularity towards the end of the nineteenth century were seen as one way of combating this damaged image. In the space of just a few months Club membership had exceeded one hundred and included both men and women. In those days none of the members were particularly skilled, most of them only slowly learning how to handle the clubs. But many, it was reported, "have already played enough to enable them to experience something of the health-giving fascination of golf."

The course was situated at the east end of the town and consisted of nine holes. What was described as "a nice little iron clubhouse" had been erected near the first tee and it was only fifteen minutes walk from the railway station and forty minutes walk from Portrush.

In the summer of 1931 a new Clubhouse at the 'old' or town course was officially opened by the Club President, Mr Montagu and in doing so he gave some interesting insights into how the game was introduced in Portstewart.

He recalled the time when there was no golf course in Portstewart and when the old course consisted only of whins, gorse and a little grass. Then a few people got together and with the advice and assistance of their friends at the Portrush Club, the first links were laid out and proved very popular.

Each year the Portrush members used to come across and play a mixed foursomes competition. They brought their lunch with them in picnic style and enjoyed themselves thoroughly. The Club progressed steadily and eventually the money was available for the construction of the splendid new course at Burnside. The Club was now in a very flourishing condition due largely, he might say, to their good secretary, Mr PH Blaikie.

The Clubhouse which this one replaced had been erected some thirty-five years earlier and for some time it had been felt that a new building was long overdue. The Club had purchased much of the ground surrounding the Clubhouse and there were plans to provide tennis courts and perhaps a bowling green as well.

At that old ceremony it was recalled, interestingly, that the first President of Portstewart Golf Club was Miss Lizzie Knox and she and a number of other founding members were present that day.

Portstewart is the home Club of Maureen Madill, a well-known commentator on golf for the BBC. She is also a member of Royal Portrush which she joined in 1968. She won the British Ladies' Amateur Championship in 1979 and the British Amateur Ladies' Stroke Play Championship the following year. In 1980 she was also a member of the Great Britain and Ireland Curtis Cup team.

When she won the British Amateur Ladies' Championship in 1979, she became the first member of the Club to do so since Miss May Hezlet's third win in 1907 and was made an honorary life member of the Club. She became a professional golfer in 1986. She is married and has been living in England for many years.

The old Royal Portrush
Golf Club

CHAPTER 30

HISTORY IN THE MAKING

It was the first competitive game of golf in Portrush

IT WAS A FAR cry from the dizzy heights of The Open in 1951, but what can be described, I think, as the first competitive game of golf in Portrush took place in the month of April in the year 1888, just a week before the formal opening of the town's newly acquired golf course.

A report of the historic match was carried in the weekly newspaper, the *Northern Constitution*, in its edition of 28 April. This is the opening paragraph:

> "Holywood has now a formidable rival in this beautiful Northern watering-place. The sand-hills or dunes which lie around it in almost every direction have been pronounced excellently suited for the enjoyment of the Royal and Ancient game."

The arranged match was something in the nature of a trial run for the new course prior to its formal opening when a party of golfers from Belfast were expected to "pay a visit to the greens to try their skill over the new country."

In that old report the observation was made also that no fewer than three separate links could, with very little outlay, be formed close to the town – one along the shore towards Portstewart, another in the direction of the Causeway and a third between the railway station and the electric tramway depot.

> "A course of nine holes has been laid out on the last-named ground. One or two of the putting runs are somewhat rough; but, taken as a whole, the sward is in first rate order. The bunker hazards (ie sandpits), unknown on the Kinnegar, afford much amusement even to the players who are unfortunate enough to get into them, while one hole placed on a plateau covered with remarkably keen turf, and a valley thirty feet deep on either side, gives capital sport to those expert with their irons."

The reporter noted that players who failed to top the hill at this hole paid the penalty "of many strokes."

The match, for a range of special prizes, had been timed to start on the arrival of the 9.05 am train from Belfast which "through the kindness of the railway company, had been accelerated for the convenience of the golfers."

The report went on to give some of the scores over this "hitherto untried and difficult ground" and they ranged from 46 to 87 strokes. The first prize was won by Mr FW Hodges, JP, from Glenravel who had played "a brilliant game."

The second round of the competition resulted in a win for Mr JS Alexander, JP, of Portglenone who carded a score of 41 net.

Between the matches, the players adjourned to the Northern Counties Hotel where "an excellent lunch was served."

The formal opening of "these interesting greens" the *Constitution* reported, would take place on Saturday 5 May. Several valuable prizes had been presented to be competed for and a large turn-out of players was expected.

This is the concluding sentence of the report:

"As golf is almost an unknown game in this part of Ireland, it is hoped that there will be a large attendance of the public to witness the interesting and lively proceedings at Portrush on Saturday next."

The first Clubhouse

CHAPTER 31

OFFICIAL PROGRAMMES –
A HIDDEN TREASURE?

Collectors were prepared to pay high prices

IF YOU HAPPEN TO have a copy of the official programme for the 1951 Open Championship then you could be sitting on a little goldmine. In fact, there were two official programmes, one covering the first two days of play, Wednesday and Thursday, and the other for Friday when two rounds were played.

I'm sure there are quite a few copies tucked away in drawers or files gathering dust in many a household so perhaps it would be worth having a look. In the world of golf memorabilia and collectibles, the 1951 Open Championship programmes are highly prized and this is reflected in the prices which collectors are prepared to pay for them.

In 2006, for example, a copy of the Wednesday/Thursday programme was sold for €1,900. It had been signed by quite a few of the leading players so that obviously added greatly to the value even though the condition, apparently, wasn't first class. Around about the same time, a copy of the programme for the 1947 Open Championship played at Hoylake and won by Fred Daly, was valued at between €700 and €900.

Many of those old programmes would, for sure, bear the signature of Max Faulkner who would doubtless have signed many after sinking his winning putt on the eighteenth green. I was there myself that day and witnessed him doing so but unfortunately I did not have a programme so I missed out badly on that score.

I have been able to look through a copy of the Wednesday/Thursday programme and it is full of interesting information. There is a section giving a short but comprehensive history of the Championship as well as a list of the winners from its inception in 1860 right up until 1950.

There are also articles giving potted histories of the Royal Portrush and Portstewart Clubs and messages of welcome and support from the Captains of both Clubs. The particular copy which I was able to examine contained the autographs of about forty of the players, including the winner, Max Faulkner, and it was in very good condition so I imagine it would be worth quite a lot of money, especially to a collector of golf memorabilia.

One of the display cabinets in the Royal Portrush Clubhouse contains pristine copies of both programmes and I was allowed to examine the Friday programme, which I had not seen before. At that time the Championship was played over three days, two rounds being played on the final day. Apart from the date I could see very little difference in the contents so I was puzzled as to why one programme had not been designed to cover the whole of the Championship.

A page of the programme was devoted to the finer points of green-keeping courtesy of a body called the Board of Green-keeping Research. It had been established in 1929 by the Joint Advisory Council of the four National Golf Unions, with the support and co-operation of the Royal and Ancient Golf Club. The object of it all was to raise turf standards through scientific research, education and advice. The Research Station was based at Bingley in Yorkshire.

A couple of pages also set out the local rules for the Royal Portrush and Portstewart Clubs with the names and length of the holes being given in each case. Maps showing the design and lay-out of the courses were included.

The programmes also contained notes for spectators who were urged to obey the stewards and see that all players got clear courses and fair play. Spectators were also warned not to pester the players for autographs and not to run on the course at any time.

There was some advertising in the programmes, notably Spalding proclaiming the merits of their "famous needled Top Flight, the world's longest and toughest ball renowned for length and durability." Saxone had a page devoted to 'Golf Master' shoes designed by Henry Cotton, the first to be designed by the player. Penfold were advertising their 'peri-dot' golf balls favoured by Dai Rees who had been elected Britain's Golfer of the Year in 1950. Bobby Locke, the defending Champion, was shown holding the famous Claret Jug in an advertisement for the Dunlop 65 golf ball.

There were also some local advertisers. The Skerry-Bhan Hotel on Landsdown Crescent was "ideally situated facing the Atlantic ocean," and had distant views of the Strand, White Rocks, Dunluce Castle and the Giant's

Causeway. The hotel had excellent facilities, including a sun-lounge and ballroom with maple floor and was within fifteen minutes of the famous Championship Golf Course. Mr and Mrs Carson were the proprietors.

In another local advertisement, John Bamford and Son were described as grocers, bakers, provision merchants and restaurant proprietors and had their business on Main Street. Bamford's Cafe served morning coffee, luncheons, teas etc, and provided efficient service and comfort.

The purchase price of the programme, incidentally, was one shilling "minimum."

Open Champion
for 2 successive years

BOBBY LOCKE
plays **Dunlop '65'**

Bobby Locke, winner of the British Open Golf Championship 1949 & 1950

A well-signed copy of the 1951 programme from Wednesday and Thursday's play, with some of the adverts found inside.

The OPEN GOLF CHAMPIONSHIP 1951

PLAYED OVER THE LINKS OF

PORTRUSH

2nd - 6th July

Official Programme
WEDNESDAY and THURSDAY

MINIMUM **1/-** PRICE

Max Faulkner's
autographed shoes.

Niall O'Boyle waits to greet
Max Faulkner with the
famous shoes.

Max Faulkner and Niall O'Boyle being interviewed for a Radio Ulster programme in 1995.

Niall O'Boyle with his souvenirs of the 1951 Open.

Causeway Street, where my mother's boarding-house was a stone's throw from the promenade.

The Billowing Sails sculpture overlooking the East Strand and promenade.

Some happy holiday makers on the last jaunting-car to be seen on the streets of Portrush in the mid-1950s.

A more modern form of transport from the same period.

My painting of White Rocks.

On the East Strand.

My view of the sixth green similar to Norman Wilkinson's famous poster for the LMS.

The Point-to-Point races at Glenvale.

In the beginning –
Portstewart Golf Club
in the early days.

The Open qualifying rounds get underway at Portstewart.

Some leading members of Rathmore Golf Club from the 1950s.

Sign at the entrance to Rathmore.

Graeme McDowell's home club.

The entrance to Rathmore Golf Club.

Side by side – Rathmore Club's badge and a pennant from Pebble Beach Club where the 2010 US Open was held.

Alan Dunbar, 2012 British Amateur Golf Champion.

The Walker Cup replica on display in Rathmore Golf Club.

The 1895 Ladies' Open Championship at Royal Portrush.

A portrait of Rhona Adair in Royal Portrush Ladies' Clubhouse.

An early view of the 'Ladies' Bathing Place' as it was known.

May Hezlet with her trophies.

Harry Colt, designer of the Royal Portrush championship course.

The card recording Rory McIlroy's record-breaking 61 on the challenging Dunluce links at Royal Portrush.

Rory McIlroy's moment of triumph in the 2011 US Open.

Replica of the US Open Championship trophy won by Graeme McDowell in 2010.

An early photograph of Graeme McDowell with some of the trophies he won as an amateur.

This montage of Graeme McDowell's 2010 US Open win hangs in Rathmore Golf Club, Portrush, his home club.

Darren Clarke with the Claret Jug.

The entrance to the Professional's shop at Royal Portrush.

The silver replica of the Claret Jug presented to the Club for safe keeping by Darren Clarke.

CHAPTER 32

HOW ABOUT A ROYALPORT GOLF SUIT?

The fitting room was surrounded by lofty mirrors

FOR THE REALLY DEDICATED and discerning golfer, it was possible at one time to purchase, only in Portrush, what was described as a very fashionable bespoke Royalport golf suit.

The White House department store on Main Street was where you could be measured for this very stylish suit, where the speciality was "high-grade tailoring in Irish tweeds at moderate prices."

An advertisement from the mid-1930s explained that the Royalport golf suit was hand-tailored throughout and that satisfaction was guaranteed. Prices were reasonable, too, starting from just £5 5s 0d.

The Portrush store was then known far and wide as "the depot for Irish peasant industries" and the proud boast was that it exported,to every country in the world, "genuine Irish Tweeds, Homespuns, Table Linen, Dress Linen, Lace, Embroideries, etc, etc."

The illustration shows one of the Royalport suits in plus-fours style and very smart it looks, too, although I'm not sure if it was meant to be worn while playing a round of golf. Perhaps it would have been for more formal occasions.

Being fitted for a bespoke suit in the White House would have been quite an experience in those days. This is an extract from an old press release:

> "The webs of the famous Irish homespuns – of which there is here an almost endless variety – are ranged vertically on the shelves at either side so that the colour and quality may be seen at a glance.
>
> "A handsome fitting room, completely surrounded by lofty mirrors, has been provided at the upper end of the establishment; while the office, where the click click of typewriters is constantly heard, has been greatly enlarged in order that the increasing correspondence

connected with the mail order section of the business may be adequately dealt with."

I'm sure the likes of Bobby Locke, Henry Cotton or Max Faulkner would have been prospective customers for one of these exclusive Royalport golf suits because at one time or another they wore plus-fours on the golf course but by 1951 the demand was probably more for "off the peg" suits and I think these hand-tailored suits might not then have been available at the White House.

DASHING AND STYLISH

The history of this type of sporting apparel has interesting links with the game of golf and it goes back to the 1920s when the new style was created – trousers that extended four inches below the knee, hence the name. It took off on the fairways in a big way with plus-fours finding a lot of favour among golfers so the White House would have been bang up to date with its Royalport suit. One observer had written: "Golfers apparently not only wanted to play well but to appear dashing and stylish."

Dashing and stylish. Those words certainly could be applied to Max Faulkner, who could be seen wearing plus-fours now and again in the 1951 Open. Even as a young boy I remember thinking how much added presence this style of clothing seemed to give him on the golf course. The plus-fours would usually be tucked into knee-length socks.

Although not so fashionable nowadays, nevertheless it still retains a measure of popularity on the golf course, particularly among professional players and one of the foremost advocates was the American, Payne Stewart, tragically killed in a plane crash in 1999 at the early age of 42. He wore plus-fours in all of his professional tournaments and he cut quite a dash because as a player he was greatly admired for having "one of the most gracefully fluid and stylish golf swings of the modern era."

CHAPTER 33

SPOTLIGHT ON A MYSTERY SHIP

The Pilgrim Steps can still be seen today

IN THE SUMMER OF 1951, a little bit of shipping history was exercising the minds of officials in Portrush. It had to do with a passenger ship which had sailed from "the Port of Rush" to America some 200 years earlier, in 1726.

That was almost exactly 100 years before Portrush had a proper harbour. In those days ships calling to pick up passengers would have dropped anchor in the bay while a ferry boat, probably a large rowing boat, pulled into the Old Dock, the older part of the harbour which is still known by that name today. Some of the "Pilgrim Steps" by which the passengers would have descended – simply half a dozen stones jutting out from the dock wall – can still be seen today also.

A query about one particular ship, unnamed, which had sailed from Portrush in the summer of 1726 had been raised by a gentleman in America, Frank E McKone by name, who had somehow discovered the names of some of the passengers.

He had written to the Ministry of Commerce seeking further information about the vessel. His letter stated:

> "It has come to my attention that a sailing vessel left the Port of Rush on August 7, 1726, arriving in Boston, Mass., on October 8 that year, with passengers from Coleraine and Ballycarry, Ireland, including John and James Harvey, and many others with their families. I am writing to learn the name of that ship and to learn the passenger list if one exists after so many years."

The Ministry had forwarded the letter to the Urban Council in Portrush requesting any information that might be available. Officials from the Ministry had already looked into the matter and had discovered, apparently, that sailing records for that period might have been kept at the Four Courts in Dublin and, that being the case, could have been lost when that building was destroyed in an explosion.

The Town Clerk of Portrush, Mr WI Cunningham, informed councillors that he had made inquiries at the local Harbour Office but no records of that period were available.

The construction of a harbour at Portrush, he pointed out, did not commence until 1827 and before that date the Old Dock was in use. Presumably as an aside to the discussion, a member of the Council, Mr J Logan, said he understood that in the early 1720s people from Portrush and Coleraine wishing to sail to Scotland would have had to depart from Ballycastle.

It would be interesting to know if that little mystery linked to the seafaring history of Portrush was ever solved. Somehow I do not think so and today it is every bit as intriguing as it was back in 1951.

AN OLD CONVICT SHIP

Portrush, of course, has a long seafaring history and down through the years ships of many shapes and sizes have dropped anchor in the harbour or close to its shores. One of the most unusual of these was surely an old convict ship named *Success*.

From an old surviving poster we learn that the ship was "the sight of a lifetime" and its visit to Portrush was probably in the summer of 1912 although there is some confusion about this. It was a museum ship and was en-route to America for an extended visit there. I think Portrush must have been its last port of call on this side of the Atlantic.

She had been fitted out for this purpose and had been touring Australian ports before heading for England. She was an impressive looking vessel of 621 tons, full masted and had been built in Burma in 1840. Some ten years later she arrived in Melbourne. It was the time of the great gold rush in Australia and the story goes that the ship's crew deserted and headed for the goldfields. At this time prisons were packed to overflowing and so the Government of Victoria tried to solve the problem by purchasing large sailing ships for use as prison hulks.

When no longer needed as a prison ship, the *Success* was bought by a group of entrepreneurs and fitted out as a museum ship, the intention being that she would travel the world, putting on display "the perceived horrors of the convict era." And that was how, one day in the summer of 1912, she sailed into Portrush. How long she stayed is not known but undoubtedly her visit must have been a big attraction for the area.

One last sad note: the *Success* fell into disrepair in the late 1930s and was destroyed by fire while being dismantled for her teak on 4 July 1946 at Cleveland, Ohio. It's interesting to know that for a while it was a unique tourist attraction in Portrush.

The newly renovated Royal Portrush clubhouse was given a Royal seal of approval in 1999 when it was officially opened by Prince Andrew. It was another memorable day in the history of the Club. Apparently Prince Andrew was so impressed with what he had seen of the famous links that he expressed an interest in perhaps returning to test it out for himself. Such an event, it was pointed out in a Press report, would be a great PR coup for the Club. Upwards of 1,000 invited guests were present as the Prince performed the opening ceremony. Many of them got to meet him personally as he went walkabout. As a memento of the occasion the Prince was presented with a watercolour painting of the celebrated sixth hole as well as a Club tie.

MAURICE McALEESE

CHAPTER 34

FRED STARTED THE BALL ROLLING AT RATHMORE

Illustrious history of a small Club

IT WOULD BE FAIR to say that when it comes to making an impact on the world stage of golf, the Rathmore Club in Portrush punches above its weight.

In its comparatively short history, for instance, it has produced two winners of Major championships. Fred Daly won The Open Championship at Hoylake in 1947 while in 2010 Graeme McDowell stormed to victory in the US Open Championship at Pebble Beach. Another Rathmore Club member, Alan Dunbar, won the British Amateur Open Championship in 2012.

The Rathmore Club is an offshoot of its close neighbour and parent club, Royal Portrush, and its roots go back to the year Fred Daly won his Championship title. It was in that year, following a meeting of the Royal Portrush Club, that permission was granted for the smaller club, which had unofficial status until then, to seek approval from the Golfing Union of Ireland to become a recognised club in its own right.

Interestingly, in those early days its members were considered as 'privileged' players and the reason for this was that approval was needed from the Royal Portrush Club before membership could be granted.

CHALLENGE OF THE VALLEY

Rathmore Club members play mostly on the adjacent Valley links course which also presents a stiff golfing challenge. I know this because I played most of my golf on the Valley but that's not a great barometer; perhaps the challenge was a lot stiffer for me than most!

In July 1953 the newly-built Rathmore Clubhouse was officially opened by Lady Babington, wife of Sir Anthony Babington, QC, who was President of the Royal Portrush Club for many years.

Six months later, in January, 1954, the first annual meeting took place and Fred Daly, who was present, was elected Captain. In a moving speech, he spoke with passion and pride, recalling his early days as a caddie and golf assistant. "I have travelled a good deal since then," he said, "won many honours but this is the greatest honour I have ever received."

He explained that travel commitments would prevent him from attending some meetings when he would be away seeking more honours but he would attend as many as he could and do everything he could for the well-being of the Club.

At that meeting some interesting statistics were quoted in relation to the construction of the Clubhouse. The sum of £450 had been raised through subscriptions and entertainments to help offset the costs. When this was added it meant that £200 was still outstanding in order to clear the debt.

Club President, Mr Jackson Taggart, was upbeat about this. When it was remembered that the building was erected but a few months ago, he felt it was a satisfactory achievement that only £200 remained outstanding.

A special finance committee had been set up to raise funds and because it was felt that the normal Club committee would now be able to handle matters, it was decided that the special committee could be disbanded.

The Rathmore Club would have to wait just over six decades before being able to fête another Major championship winner from within its ranks in the person of Graeme McDowell, a worthy winner of the US Open Championship in 2010.

Another young Rathmore player who is making a name for himself is Alan Dunbar, the 2012 British Open Amateur Champion and a Walker Cup player in 2011. He has now turned professional. Wayne Telford, a gifted amateur also turned professional, is another Rathmore name to watch out for.

Portraits of all these players hang proudly in the Rathmore Clubhouse and looking around on a recent visit I was soon caught up in the echoes not only of the history of this remarkable Club but also the history of Portrush itself.

PRIVILEGED HISTORY

During the course of my visit I was given a copy of a book detailing the history of the Club, *Privileged Players – The Story of Rathmore Golf Club, Portrush… so far.*

It is dedicated to the memory of Dermot McNally, one of the co-authors, who sadly died before the book was completed. In the preface, Club President Rory Hamilton, also one of the authors, described Dermot as "the driving force behind the early fashioning of this history."

In a chapter entitled 'The Early Years', Dermot explains succinctly just how the Privileged Players club came into being, observing:

> "The appeal and fascination of golf inspired several of the locals to participate in this new sport which had come to their town."

Eventually, at times when the new course was not so busy, residents could play at a reduced fee. In time, as a gesture of goodwill, as Dermot wrote, limited associate membership was offered to enthusiastic local male residents. A Town/Residents Club was formed for Privileged Players and so it remained until the formation of Rathmore Golf Club in 1947.

Others who had a hand in the writing of the Rathmore book were Patsy Cahill, Hugo Finlay and JA Taggart.

THE STORY SO FAR

It was absolutely right that the words "so far" should be added to the book's sub-title because more golfing greatness will surely emerge from this place. The Clubhouse walls and trophy cabinets are brimming with inspiration for would-be champions of the future.

For example, one of the most impressive of the trophies is Graeme McDowell's US Open Championship Cup, or rather a fine replica of it, commemorating his great win at Pebble Beach in 2010.

Then there is a replica of the Walker Cup which commemorates the participation of McDowell and Dunbar in this prestigious team event. In 2001 Graeme was a member of the Great Britain and Ireland team which beat the USA by 15 points to 9 at Ocean Forest Golf Club, Sea Island, Georgia. Ten years later, in 2011, Alan was on the Great Britain and Ireland team which beat the USA by 14 points to 12 when the match was played at Royal Aberdeen Golf Club in Scotland.

I'll just finish off with this little story from the book. It's from the section entitled 'Odds and Ends':

> "In February 2005, Graeme McDowell met Darren Clarke in the first round of the Accenture Match Play Championship at La Costa,

California. This is a World Championship event. Darren's father, Godfrey, was at the time the popular Captain of Rathmore, while Graeme's father, Kenny, was a popular member of the Rathmore Committee. Naturally there must have been divided loyalties in the Club's membership. In the event, Graeme triumphed on the final green, which was the only time he led in this match between two firm friends."

More golfing greatness will surely emerge from this place.

CHAPTER 35

PORTRUSH GIRL MADE GOLFING HISTORY

There were amazing scenes of celebration and jubilation

THE WELCOME GIVEN TO Fred Daly when he returned to Portrush with the famed Claret Jug in 1947 was tremendous but it did not compare to that given to a young girl from the town when she returned home with *two* Championship trophies on a warm summer night at the turn of the last century.

There were amazing scenes of jubilation and celebration. It seemed as if the entire population had turned out and you could almost feel the high state of anticipation and excitement that hung in the warm night air. They were awaiting the arrival of a train carrying this young lady who had taken the golfing world by storm. She had brought off a unique double in the history of ladies' golf by winning two major championships in the space of just two weeks.

The local heroine was May Hezlet, and as the train she and her mother were travelling in pulled slowly into the station the night sky was suddenly illuminated by an explosion of fireworks, surely a sound and a sight that left them in no doubt as to the type of welcome that awaited them.

The year was 1899 and the girl from Portrush had won the Ladies' Open Championship held under the auspices of the Ladies' Golfing Union of the United Kingdom, shortly after winning the Irish Ladies' Open Championship, both played at Newcastle. It was claimed that, at seventeen, this made her one of the youngest champions in the history of golf. Her double success received huge press coverage. She was hailed by one writer as "a courageous and skilful player," her capture of the double crown being immensely popular.

In The Open Championship there had been a strong contingent of players from England and the Irish contestants were not expected to make much of an impact. As it turned out, eleven of the 25 Irish players in the field progressed to the third round; four reached the fourth round; three got through to the fifth and two to the semi-finals, both reaching the final – Miss

Hezlet and Miss Magill from County Down, the reigning champion. This is a brief description of the play:

"The weather was magnificent, and there was a brilliant muster of spectators. Miss Hezlet was pretty closely held up to the eleventh hole, but the match was square at the thirteenth, and then she played steadily and brilliantly all the way home. She won the 14th, halved the 15th, won the 16th, and divided the 17th – thus winning the match and The Open Championship by 2 up and 1 to play."

In the final of the Irish Ladies' Championship Miss Hezlet beat Miss Rhona Adair (Killymoon) 5 up and 4 to play.

It was a truly remarkable achievement. For Mary Elizabeth Linzee Hezlet (May) it was surely a dream come true and in the midst of that ecstatic welcome she must have been thinking back to the day when, as an eager eleven-year-old, she tried out her first set of golf clubs on the Royal Portrush links under the watchful eye of her mother.

Even then she probably displayed some of the natural talent and flair that would take her to the pinnacle of success and ensure an enduring place for her in the early annals of golfing history. Writing about her 1899 achievements, one golf correspondent observed:

"Miss Hezlet has acquired wonderful judgement within a remarkably short period; and, aided by a strong physique, plays the game admirably in all its points. She was the runner-up in last year's Irish Ladies Golf Championship tournament at Malone and was only beaten by a putt on the last hole; while for some time past she has won most of the scratch medals offered by the Royal Portrush Club."

At the time she also held the record for the ladies' course at Portrush – 77. And she had gone round the tough men's course in 95 strokes.

When the sound of fireworks had died down that summer night in Portrush, a loud cheer went up as the young golfing star and her mother emerged from the railway station. They were greeted by a welcoming party which included leading members of the Royal Portrush Club and she was presented with a large bouquet. Then, to the sound of a flute band from Coleraine, they were escorted to an open carriage drawn by four smart horses waiting in readiness just outside the station.

They were joined in the carriage by Colonel Pottinger and Mr JS Alexander,

DL, of Royal Portrush but before the entourage moved off, there was a last-minute change of plan; horse-power was dispensed with. The horses were unhitched and instead, "willing hands" pulled the carriage along Mark Street and Main Street to Rock Ryan, followed by the cheering crowds while the band played "lively airs." This is an extract from *The Northern Constitution* report:

> "Opposite the Northern Counties Hotel, Colonel Pottinger, as Captain of the Club, on behalf of Miss Hezlet, thanked the people for the magnificent reception they had given her. At Rock Ryan fire rockets were again discharged, and a bonfire was lighted on the salmon green. Later in the evening, in the presence of a large crowd, Captain Watt, chairman of the Urban Council, in the name of the town, congratulated Miss Hezlet on the double victory she had won as a golfer, conferring distinction not only on herself but on Portrush and her country. Colonel Hezlet appropriately acknowledged the compliment."

It was surely a night to remember not only for May Hezlet and her family, but also for the crowds of residents and visitors. In keeping with the protocol of the times, no doubt, the young champion did not speak herself at that great reception. Her father, Colonel Hezlet, and the Club Captain, did so on her behalf. Perhaps her tender age had something to do with it as well.

May Hezlet lived until the ripe old age of 95 and it is fascinating to think that she would have been among the crowds of spectators at The Open Championship in 1951 and would have followed the play with an avid interest. What a pity some enterprising reporter did not obtain an interview. It would have been well worth reading.

"Miss May Hezlet, who carried off the Ladies' Championship and the Irish Ladies' Championship in successive weeks at Newcastle, County Down, when she was only seventeen, and who altogether won the Ladies' Championship thrice and the Irish title five times, occupied much the same position in ladies' golf in the first decade of the present century as was later on accorded in turn to Miss Cecil Leith and Miss Joyce Wethered, and there is no doubt her example did a lot to raise the standard of ladies' play in those important early days."

From an old edition of the Royal Portrush Club's
official handbook published in the late 1950s

CHAPTER 36

HARRY PUTS STAMP ON ROYAL PORTRUSH

He considered it his finest achievement

Back in the 1930s, when the foremost golf course architect of the day, HS (Harry) Colt stood back and surveyed what he had achieved in his new lay-out and design for Royal Portrush Club's Dunluce championship links, he was more than satisfied. In fact, he considered it his finest achievement.

However, it was still a 'split' course, with the first and last holes, along with the Clubhouse, sited on the large triangle of town-locked land, cut off from the seaward section by the busy main road from Portrush to Bushmills.

It was the ultimate aim of the Club to leave this road-bounded triangle area altogether, thus having the whole of the course laid out in one magnificent sweep dipping in and out of sand-dunes bounded on one side by East Strand with players no longer having to contend with an intersecting highway.

That development, however, did not happen for another decade or so when a site suitable for a new Clubhouse was acquired and a hotel which stood on it converted for the purpose. It meant that the old triangle part of the course could now be abandoned with the first and last holes beginning and ending at the new Clubhouse. Again Colt was called in to help with the modified design and lay-out.

Even after whatever alterations need to be made to facilitate the modern day requirements of The Open, the course will still bear the stamp of Harry Colt's magical touch.

It's interesting that within five or six years of this major development in the mid-1940s, The Open Championship was being played on its majestic fairways for the first time. Mr Colt would surely have been delighted. Sadly he died in November 1951.

At the opening of the new course in 1933, Club President Anthony Babington KC, MP (later Sir Anthony Babington) said he did not think it was rivalled by anything they had in Ireland at present. He thought it was not too much to say that, especially in the way the beauties of nature had been taken advantage of, their new course ought in a year or two to become one of the foremost in the Kingdom.

The work had cost some £3,200 and had provided employment for thirty workmen. Even before the official opening it had been played over by some of the members and they had given it the thumbs up. In a report of the opening ceremony, the *Coleraine Chronicle* noted:

> "The event was not only of outstanding interest in the life of the popular holiday resort, but also one of no small importance in the history of Irish golfing progress."

TEE-BOX FOR THE LORD MAYOR

Performing the ceremony was the Lord Mayor of London, Sir Percy Greenaway and the second tee 'Greenaway' was named in his honour. Today, somewhere in the Lord Mayor's Mansion House in London there is an inscribed silver replica of the tee-box marking the hole. It was presented to the Lord Mayor as a memento of the occasion.

In a comment on the practice of giving individual names to golf holes, the *Chronicle* correspondent pointed out that although most golf course nomenclature was of a colloquial type, the Club was pursuing "a more serious" form of naming and gave the example of 'Hughie', which was the name of one hole on the course in appreciation of the efforts of the Club's popular head green-keeper, Hugh McNeill, who took charge of the laying of the new greens and was largely instrumental "in achieving their remarkably forward condition."

Interestingly, a second 18-hole course (The Valley) running alongside the Dunluce links was under construction and was expected to be completed shortly. Fourteen holes had already been finished. It occupied a portion of the ladies' old course and a portion of the former championship course and would be used by players of both sexes.

A NEW BEGINNING

June 1947 saw the opening of the newly acquired and renovated Clubhouse and the VIP doing the honours this time was the Governor of Northern Ireland, Earl Granville.

In welcoming the Governor the Club Captain, Lt-Colonel CO Hezlet, said they had a first class course and in due time would have a first class Clubhouse, adding, significantly, that they hoped to be able to arrange for either the British Open amateur or the British Open Championship to be played at Portrush.

In time-honoured manner, the Governor, who was "a great sportsman and a good golfer" made an excellent tee shot with a club presented to him by the Club professional, PG Stevenson. The *Chronicle* reported:

> "Dozens of caddies, well out on the fairway, scrambled for the ball, and the caddie who retrieved it, John Bacon, received a gift of £1 from the Governor."

Royal Portrush caddies were set an unusual but exciting challenge involving no less a personage than the Lord Mayor of London one day in the summer of 1933. Sir Percy Greenaway was in Portrush to declare open the redesigned Dunluce links course. In doing so, Sir Percy was obliged to hit a drive from the first tee, an old tradition apparently.

To add interest, caddies were tasked with retrieving the ball and in order to do so dozens of them took up strategic positions along the first hole, many of them in the rough it must be said. That must have been a bit off-putting for Sir Percy because he fluffed his drive.

As noted in the *Coleraine Chronicle*: "After a few practice swings, Sir Percy, who wore an orthodox golfing jacket, sliced his drive into the rough and smilingly remarked: 'With that magnificent effort I formally open your new course. I hope every player who comes after me will drive a better ball than I did.' The caddy who retrieved the ball, Eddie Magee, was rewarded 'in the traditional manner'."

A 1951 view of the Golf Club

CHAPTER 37

NEW COURSE ON WESTERN FRONT

...there was intense interest in the game

A FTER THE HISTORIC OPEN Championship in Portrush in 1951, it's safe to assume there was an upsurge in the number of people taking up the game, not only in and around Portrush but also in the Province as a whole. Perhaps some might even have fancied themselves as the next Fred Daly, although five or six decades would have to elapse before that happened with the emergence of Graeme McDowell and Darren Clarke.

There was an intense interest in the game following its introduction to this part of the world in the latter end of the nineteenth century. In the summer of 1895, for example, considerable excitement was aroused with the opening of a new golf course at Dhu Varren, on a fringe of hills overlooking the resort's picturesque western shoreline.

It was a nine-hole golf course and this is how the opening was reported in the *Coleraine Chronicle*:

"The Dhu Varren golf course was formally opened on Monday, when a competition took place for a prize presented by Mr WJ Morrow, one of the joint owners of the ground. Very rarely, however, has rain fallen with such wholehearted copiousness as it did on that afternoon. Competitors were consequently few and, needless to add, they were drenched.

"Dr Creery, Coleraine, did the course in 55, and carried off the prize, Dr Carson, Portrush being second with but one point less. As may be supposed, the holes are all rather short, except the eighth; but the hazards are numerous, and the greens are such as to tax the skill of the cunningest player. Plenty of play will greatly improve the ground."

Sounds like it was a case of 'just what the doctor ordered' when that opening round was played!

The following week the new course would have been given a really good test by a group of competitors who would have known quite a lot about golf – caddies. In the news columns of the *Northern Constitution* it was announced:

> "Next week there will be an interesting golf competition on the Dhu Varren links – the new golf course between the railway line and the west strand. The intending competitors are the caddies who attend players on the links of the Royal Portrush Golf Club, and an English hunting watch is the trophy for which they will compete.
>
> "We should add that Mr Morrow's new links opened last week with a spirited competition for a nice prize which was won by Dr JT Creery, Coleraine, the runner-up being Dr TH Carson, Portrush. The weather was wet but this was unheeded by the players, who stuck to their course as true golfers always do – in spite of wind or weather. Experienced players pronounce the new links perfectly satisfactory."

I wonder how long that little golf course remained in use. It can't have been too long because quite a lot of development took part in that part of Portrush and today it's hard to imagine that it existed at all. I was interested to learn how the caddies got on in that match and which of them won the English hunting watch but I was not able to turn anything up.

CADDIES TO THE FORE

However, I did come across another interesting item relating to caddies shortly after the turn of the last century. By this time I think that little nine-hole course at Dhu Varren would not have been still going but I can't be sure. Anyway, this particular competition for caddies was organised by the Royal Portrush Club and I think it must have been a regular fixture.

It's nice to be able to record the names of some of the caddies who did such sterling work on the Portrush golf links in the olden days when golf trolleys had not been thought of.

In its 'Local News' column the *Coleraine Chronicle* reported that the Council of the Royal Portrush Golf Club had arranged a couple of competitions for caddies (senior and junior) and these were brought to a conclusion on Saturday with very satisfactory results.

The senior competition was held on the long course and that for juniors on the ladies' links. The results were:

Senior Caddies – James Edmundson (winner of scratch prize) 81; John Taylor (winner of 1st handicap prize after a tie) 84; George Martin (winner of 2nd handicap prize) 94; Joseph Harvey (scr.) 86; Frederick Mann (6) 92; George Rankin (6) 94; Hugh Rankin (9) 97; John Hamill (4) 96; Hugh Kelly (scr.) 93.

Junior Caddies – D Thompson (1st scratch prize) 75; J Todd (1st handicap prize) (8) 83; G Hamill (2nd handicap prize) (9) 89; P McGratton (9) 90; J Martin (9) 91; J Thompson (9) 91; H McGratton (8) 92.

CHAPTER 38

BERNARD'S PEN WAS MIGHTY

...the course is truly magnificent

RENOWNED GOLF WRITER BERNARD Darwin was in Portrush in 1951 writing about the Open Championship for *The Times* newspaper. It was his first visit to Portrush and his first sight of the much acclaimed Dunluce links. This is an extract from an article he wrote for *The Times* on 3 July:

"The first Open Championship ever to be held in Ireland was begun at Portrush yesterday, and I must to my shame confess that I have never before seen this grand course. Let me at once pay it my respectful compliments.

"It is truly magnificent and Mr HS Colt, who designed it in its present form, has thereby built himself a monument more enduring than brass. This Course does not disdain the spectacular, such as the one-shot hole called Calamity Corner, with its terrifying sandy cliffs and its gadarene descent into unknown depths to the right of the green; for the most part the course does not depend on any such dramatic quality, but rather on the combined soundness and subtlety of the architecture.

"There is a constant demand for accuracy of driving, the more so at present as the rough is really worthy of its name and the approaches are full of varied interest. In particular there are one or two holes of the despised length called 'a drive and a pitch' which are entirely fascinating, such as the fifth, with its green almost on the brink of the sea, and the 15th. The greens are full of interesting undulations and altogether I find it hard to imagine a more admirable test of golf."

That was praise indeed, coming from a man who had written so extensively about the 'Golden Age' of golf – he started writing for *The Times* in 1907 and continued to do so until 1953. A grandson of the naturalist Charles Darwin, he had the distinction of being the first person ever to cover golf on a daily basis. He was also a contributor for *Country Life* from 1907 until 1961, the year he died.

On top of this he wrote dozens of books and some of them, such as *Golf Courses of the British Isles* (1910), *A History of Golf in Great Britain* (1910) and *Hints on Golf* (1912) are much sought after by collectors. His book *Bernard Darwin on Golf* comes high on the list of the best books ever written about the game, which he played himself to a high level as an amateur.

HOPE SPRINGS ETERNAL

According to one source, his prose was composed "with such a fine eye" that he was often referred to as the greatest golf writer – some would say sports writer – of all time. He wrote:

> "How grateful we golfers ought to be that our game will last us almost as long as we last ourselves and that hope can still spring eternally in our ridiculous breasts."

The American golfer, Ben Crenshaw, said of him: "One can open a book by Bernard Darwin at any page, find any line, and be entertained by it."

Although no mean golfer himself, in his case it could be truly said that his pen was mightier than his club, the finest writer, it was claimed on the cover of one of his books, "ever to elevate the discussion of golf beyond a simple reportage of events." In 2005 he was elected to the World Golf Hall of Fame in the Lifetime Achievement category.

Recently I was fortunate enough to obtain a copy of Bernard Darwin's book *The Golf Courses of the British Isles* and I thought I had come across a real treasure. It was not, however, the original 1910 copy but a facsimile which, I suppose, might be rare enough nowadays. The book is beautifully illustrated with some sixty-four watercolour paintings by Harry Rountree, a very talented artist, and I would have bought it for these alone.

The one of Portrush is of the seventeenth green and from the sweep of sandhills part of the East Strand can be seen with a headland of some houses and the salmon fishery in the background. He gives a short description of the Royal Portrush links, the lay-out of which would have been much different from today because in 1933 the course had been completely redesigned by Harry Colt.

THE GAME WITH THE HOLE IN IT

Another great golf writer who would have been in Portrush for the 1951 Open was Peter Dobereiner who died in 1997. He was widely regarded as one of the greatest golf writers the sport has ever seen and was said to be "a much loved personality throughout the golf world."

One of the books he wrote is called, *The Game with the Hole in it*, published in 1973. In a review in the *Guardian*, Pat Ward-Thomas declared:

> "Rarely does one come across a golfing book that sustains interest throughout, entertains and stimulates thought. One such is The Game with the Hole in it. His writing has inventiveness of phrase and a dry sense of humour..."

In the introduction to the book, the author states:

> "The book, I hope, is more like a game of golf itself – a leisurely stroll with occasional halts for business but without ever forgetting, as the great American golfer Walter Hagen insisted, to smell the flowers along the way."

I have an interesting little story of my own to tell about that book as well. While browsing in a charity shop one day I spotted a copy and bought it for the princely sum of 50p. Later when I was checking the internet for some information relating to golf I discovered that it is listed in the top twenty best books ever written about the game. Not only that, it was said to be a "hard to find volume" nowadays and that if you come across it you should snap it up. That's what I did and it now sits alongside Bernard Darwin's volume in my bookcase.

CHAPTER 39

RORY'S STUNNING ROUND

A 61 – and it could have been better!

S OME OF THE WORLD's best golfers converged on Portrush in 1951 to try
and win the world's most prestigious golf title, The Open Championship,
being staged over the Royal Portrush Club's famous Dunluce links for the
very first time.

Predictions were that a new course record could well be established and
sure enough it happened – a 66 posted by Jack Hargreaves, Sutton Coldfield,
one stroke better than Bobby Locke's 67.

No one then would have dared to predict, I'm sure, that just over half-a-
century later this record would have been reduced by some five shots to just
61. And not by a top professional golfer but by a 16-year-old schoolboy!

It is one of the best, if not the best, rounds of golf ever produced on the
tough Dunluce Championship course and the schoolboy who achieved this
phenomenal round was none other than Rory McIlroy.

He did it while competing in the North of Ireland Amateur Championship
in 2005, a competition held each year on the Portrush links. Admittedly,
the course may have undergone some changes in the years between but the
standard scratch score was still the same at 72.

The card he returned that day is on display in one of the Club's trophy
cabinets, a tangible reminder of a superb round of golf conducted
with symphonic grace and style by an amazing young player who was
comparatively unknown at the time. Here are the figures for that round:

Out – 4, 4, 3, 4, 4, 2, 4, 4, 4 – 33
In – 3, 2, 4, 4, 2, 3, 3, 4, 3 – 28

"To shoot a 61 anywhere is great," he said in a press interview afterwards,
"but to shoot it around Royal Portrush is even better."

It was a score that could have been even lower because he just missed a six-foot putt for birdie on the first green. Looking back, he told reporters: "I turned on three under, birdied 9, eagled 10, birdied 11, parred 12 and 13 and then birdied my way in. Basically I didn't miss a shot from then on." It was just one of those days, he declared, when "everything is on song."

It was only the third occasion that he had played the Dunluce links. As the *Coleraine Chronicle* noted:

> "…undoubtedly the highlight of the Championship was the fantastic new course record 61 from Holywood teenager Rory McIlroy. In fact, not only did he better the previous best of 64 by Randall Evans, he smashed it with nine birdies and an eagle in a flawless round on the Dunluce course."

The Portrush air obviously agreed with him. He added a round of 71 over the Valley course to lead the qualifiers with a total of 132, five shots clear of the nearest challenger, R Cannon from Balbriggan. Those who witnessed that round of golf probably realised they were watching the blossoming of a future star who would soon be making his presence felt on the world stage of golf. And they were not wrong.

As everyone now knows, they did not have long to wait. Within two years this young man from Holywood had joined the professional ranks and just four years later, in 2011, was holding aloft the coveted US Open Championship trophy. He had won the title at the Congressional County Club in Maryland by a massive margin of eight shots, sixteen under par 268 for the four rounds. It was acclaimed as one of sport's greatest achievements. A photograph commemorating this moment of triumph hangs in the Royal Portrush Clubhouse.

The only possible way this brilliant young player could come close to capping that was by winning The Open itself and, of course, he did that in some style at Hoylake, venue for the 2014 Championship, emulating the feat of Portrush hero Fred Daly, who also won the title at Hoylake in 1947.

After his record-breaking round at Royal Portrush in 2005, he went on to become the youngest ever winner of both the West of Ireland Championship and the Irish Close Championship. After his US Open win, Rory paid tribute to his great friend Graeme McDowell who had won the same tournament the previous year. "If Graeme had not won last year," he said, "I don't think I would be standing here talking to you as a Major champion."

Just weeks after winning the Open at Hoylake, he went on to win another Major title, the US PGA Championship at Valhalla which he had also won in 2012. Now a four-time Major champion and without doubt the world's best golfer, McIlroy has his sights firmly set on golf's the US Masters in 2015. Victory here would give him a personal Grand Slam (winner of all four Major titles). He still regards the Ryder Cup, however, in which he has distinguished himself so well, as "the best tournament in the world."

Apart from that personal ambition, it means that Northern Ireland has now produced four Major golf champions starting with Fred Daly in 1947. With The Open set to return to Portrush in the course of the next few years, it's obviously a major boost for golf in this part of the world. Royal Portrush is sometimes described as the spiritual home of golf in Northern Ireland. So it's hard to argue against the claim that Portrush is also, as proclaimed on roadside placards in and around the town bearing the names of Fred Daly, Graeme McDowell and Darren Clarke, that it is the 'Major Golf Capital of the World'.

Six months after winning the US title, Rory McIlroy was awarded an MBE in the New Year Honours list.

-MAURICE McALEESE-

CHAPTER 40

GRAEME'S REMARKABLE STORY

And it's still unfolding

SOME PEOPLE IN THE huge crowd gathered in and around Rathmore Golf Club on a warm evening in the summer of 2010 were recollecting how a young boy, years earlier, had learned to play the game on the Club's nine-hole pitch and putt course.

So there was a little bit of nostalgia in the air as they waited to greet that youngster, now a young man of 30, on his arrival at the Club just days after he had won the US Open Championship, one of the world's great golf tournaments.

Graeme McDowell was the toast of the town and, indeed, the whole country. He had taken the golf world by storm, leaving some of the best players the game has ever seen, trailing in his wake to claim his first Major championship title at Pebble Beach in the California sunshine.

No one who had witnessed his first tentative swings on that little pitch and putt course could have imagined the glittering career that lay ahead. Perhaps there would have been more of an inkling of this when he began to play on the Club's testing Valley links or on the nearby Dunluce championship links of Royal Portrush.

Stylish and charismatic, both on and off the golf course, McDowell was proud of his Portrush roots. His stunning victory had put the media spotlight firmly on this small seaside town. Its credentials as a world-class golfing venue were being spread far and wide.

That initial homecoming party, with the media 'circus' in tow, lasted well into the small hours. Many fine tributes were paid and more would follow over the next few weeks in a more intimate and relaxed reception. Graeme McDowell seemed to take it all in his stride. In a press interview he said:

> "I'm sure I've surprised some people but I hope I haven't surprised everyone. I hope that people know enough about my game to know that hopefully the win at Pebble Beach wasn't a fluke."

He described his victory as a dream and "the fulfilment of everything I have put into the game for most of my life." He was glad that his father, Kenny, had been at his side in his moment of triumph at Pebble Beach, more especially because it was Father's Day.

So the sound of ball dropping to the bottom of the cup as he sank his last putt was one that surely echoed down the corridors of golfing history. Here, acknowledging the eruption of cheers and applause, stood the first golfer from Northern Ireland to win this Major championship.

One of the people who would not have been too surprised at his victory was close friend, Rory McIlroy, who turned up unexpectedly at Rathmore for that homecoming welcome. He said: "I have played a lot of golf with G-Mac over the years and to see what he has done gives me a lift."

Prophetically, he added that he had played golf with his friend enough times to realise that he could go out on any given week and "do the same thing." Little did he realise then that US Open glory was beckoning for him also because, of course, he went on to win the Championship the very next year.

FOLLOWING IN MIGHTY FOOTSTEPS

But 2010 belonged to Graeme McDowell. He had won the US Championship on one of the great golf courses of America. Perhaps he would have known what Jack Nicklaus had said about it:

> "If I had only one more round to play, I would chose to play it at Pebble Beach. I've loved this course from the first time I saw it. It's possibly the best in the world."

I don't think he ever played the Dunluce links at Royal Portrush.

Another interesting fact about Pebble Beach – it has hosted the US Open on five occasions and will do so again in 2019.

Graeme McDowell had shown in 2010 that this spectacular ocean-side course suited his game to a tee. Now he was back in his native Portrush to share his history-making achievement with family and friends and a legion of fans. Nothing like it had been seen in Portrush since 1947 when the great Fred Daly had returned to his birthplace with the famous Claret Jug after his momentous victory in the Open Golf Championship at Hoylake, the first Irishman to win the trophy.

McDowell was following in mighty footsteps. Congratulations had been pouring in from all sections of the community, all spectrums of the political divide, including the First and Deputy First Ministers, Peter Robinson and Martin McGuinness, united in their praise of a sporting achievement that had sent such positive images of Northern Ireland across the globe.

This young man's triumphant homecoming as the US Open Golf Champion surely ranks as one of the most memorable in the sporting history of Portrush and Rathmore Golf Club. The pride and the joy were captured best by Colin Walker, who was then Club Captain, when he declared:

> "It's hard to believe that Graeme started out on the pitch-and-putt behind us and is now bringing back the US Open Championship trophy."

Today there is a space in the Club car-park permanently reserved for the 2010 US Open Champion and on an outside wall a notice proclaims a similar message letting you know that this is the home Club of Graeme McDowell. In case you miss that there is also an attractive panel above the main entrance with the same proclamation but with the addition of two colour photographs.

Inside the Clubhouse, in one of the display cabinets, there is a replica of the magnificent trophy, another permanent reminder of the day the Club's most celebrated member made golfing history on the far side of the Atlantic. You are very much aware of this moment in time, beautifully portrayed in several magnificent colour photographs which adorn the walls.

My eye was drawn, however, to a much smaller, black and white photograph of Graeme, looking not much older, perhaps, than when he started out all those years ago on the Club's pitch and putt course.

He has, of course, a proud record in the Ryder Cup having made four appearances in this prestigious event. Incidentally, Fred Daly was the first Irishman to play in the Ryder Cup, having achieved that accolade in 1947, the year he won the Open Championship.

After his triumph in the US Open, Graeme McDowell was given honorary life membership of Royal Portrush Golf Club. In 2011 he was awarded the MBE in the New Year Honours for services to golf. In June of the same year he received an honorary Doctorate from the University of Ulster for services to golf.

It really is a remarkable story. And it's still unfolding.

CHAPTER 41

OPEN DELIGHT: DARREN BRINGS HOME THE CLARET JUG

It was a magical time for golf in Northern Ireland

WHEN DARREN CLARKE ARRIVED back in Portrush with the world's best known golf trophy, the Claret Jug, after his great victory in the 2011 Open Golf Championship at Royal St George's in Kent, he would have been well aware that he was turning back the pages of history. The last time the trophy had been seen in Portrush was in 1951 when the Royal Portrush Club hosted the Championship. Max Faulkner was the winner then.

The last time it had been brought back in triumph to Portrush was four years earlier than that, in 1947 when it was won by Fred Daly at Hoylake. Now, in 2011, the story was being repeated and it was Darren Clarke's footsteps striding majestically down the fairways of history.

It was a magical time for golf in Northern Ireland. Portrush man Graeme McDowell had started the ball rolling in 2010, winning the US Open Championship at Pebble Beach in California. Just a year later the same Championship was won by Holywood's Rory McIlroy and in that year also Darren Clarke from Dungannon, but now living in Portrush, had come following through, winning The Open Championship and setting up a trio of triumphs in Major golf tournaments that is surely unique in the history of the game in this small corner of the world.

In his bid to win the most famous of all the Major championships, Clarke had shown great spirit and determination as well as superb skill. It was a dream he had pursued doggedly over a period of some twenty years and now the dream had come true.

Along the way, his career as a professional golfer had its highs and lows but although there were more highs than lows, the famous Claret Jug, most coveted of all golf trophies, had eluded him. Until now.

So there was great rejoicing not only in Portrush but all over Northern Ireland when he arrived back in the Province, his name carved with pride on this most famous of golf trophies, its origins spanning virtually the entire history of the Royal and Ancient game itself.

When the last putt rolled in on the 18th green at Royal St George's the first emotional hugs were from his mum and dad, Hetty and Godfrey, and his then fiancée, Alison Campbell (now his wife) as he claimed the title to become Northern Ireland's third Major championship winner in just over a year. Five years earlier, in 2006, he had lost his wife Heather to breast cancer so it was a moment tinged with a little sadness. In his acceptance speech Darren paid a moving tribute to his late wife and his two young sons, Tyrone and Conor. The boys had been watching the unfolding drama on television with other relatives at their home in Portrush and they were his first priority when he arrived back home with the trophy.

Over the next few days and weeks there were celebrations with friends and family, press interviews, receptions and welcome home parties. One of the abiding images is of the newly crowned champion on the balcony of Royal Portrush Golf Club with his two sons, holding aloft the spoils of victory.

One of the most popular winners of this famous trophy in modern times, his success had thrown a blanket of delight across the whole of the country. First Minister Peter Robinson caught the mood when he declared: "Scotland may be the spiritual home of golf but Northern Ireland is unquestionably home to the world's best golfers."

Darren Clarke had, according to the Deputy First Minister, Martin McGuinness, conducted himself with a grace and determination that was nothing short of outstanding.

"A person with great dreams can achieve great things." That is a quotation from a book by one of America's top golfing performance consultants, Dr Bob Rotella. It's called *Golf is not a Game of Perfect* and recently I was lucky enough to acquire a copy of the British edition. It is a really good read even for someone with just a passing interest in golf. And what better recommendation could it have: the foreword is written by Darren Clarke.

INDEX

O'Connor, Christy, 101
Palladium Ballroom, 87, 89
Park, William, 16
Patton, Hughie, 92
Pebble Beach, 83, 134, 136, 153-154, 156
Pennink, Frank, 38, 49, 101
Peters, Larry, 36
Picture House, The, 64, 11
Pinehurst, 14
Porter, Harry, 97
Portrush Advertising Committee, 41, 159
Portrush Lily, The, 58-60
Portrush Pipe Band, 35
Portstewart Golf Club, 17, 80, 120-123
Pottinger, Colonel, 139-140
Poulson, Alan 'Tiger', 26
Prestwick Golf Club, 16
Ramage, Mr, 56-57
Ramore Hill, 35
Rathmore Club, 7, 12, 134-137, 153-155
Rees, Dai, 107, 117, 127
Rosapenna, 29
Ross, LV, 58, 59
Rotella, Bob, 157
Rountree, Harry, 148
Route Harriers, 34
Royal Aberdeen Golf Club, 136
Royal Belfast Golf Club, 20
Royal County Down, 15, 76
Royal Liverpool, 60, 159
Royalport golf suit, 129-130
Royal Portrush Hotel, 32
Ryder Cup, 100, 107, 152, 155
Scott, Lady Margaret, 13

Shankland, Bill, 100, 107
Shutt, WR, 33, 63, 109
Simons, Harry, 109-110
Simpson, HF, 16
Skerries, The, 40, 55, 84
Skerry-Bhan Hotel, 31, 33, 127
Snead, Sam, 12
Stevens, Frances (Bunty), 61
Stevenson, PG, 143
Stewart, Conne, 36
Stewart, Payne, 130
Storer-Carson, JA, 37, 101
Stranahan, Frank, 35, 136
Taggart, Jackson, 135, 136
Tarry Burn, 57
Telford, Wayne, 135
Traill, Dr Anthony, 28
Traill, William Acheson, 28, 69
Ulster Scratch Cup, 61, 62
Ulster Tourist Association, 45
Ulster Transport Authority, 45, 91, 102
Valhalla, 152
van Donk, Florrie, 72
Vardon, Harry, 13, 29-30, 60
Vint, Charles, 77-78
von Nida, Norman, 107
Walker, Colin, 155
Walker Cup, 135, 136
Ward, Charlie, 100
Webster, Leila, 36
Westward Ho, 14
Wethered, Joyce, 13-14, 140
White House, The, 86, 129-130
White Rocks, 27, 31, 69, 75, 84, 119, 127
Wilkinson, Norman, 118, 119
Willis, Joan, 36